The Black Death

*An Enthralling Overview of a Major Event
in the Middle Ages*

Free limited time bonus

Stop for a moment. We have a free bonus set up for you. The problem is this: we forget 90% of everything that we read after 7 days. Crazy fact, right? Here's the solution: we've created a printable, 1-page pdf summary for this book that you're reading now. All you have to do to get your free pdf summary is to go to the following website:

https://livetolearn.lpages.co/enthrallinghistory/

Once you do, it will be intuitive. Enjoy, and thank you!

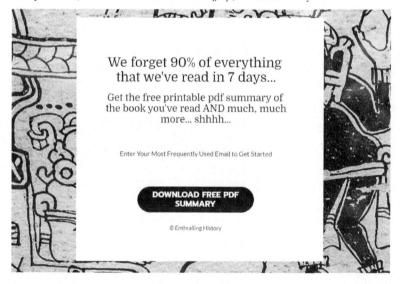

Table of Contents

Introduction

As the world begins to emerge from the recent pandemic, many might struggle to imagine a more deadly disease. However, back in the 1300s, a pandemic known as the Black Death began spreading throughout Asia, Europe, and North Africa, and for many, contraction was fatal. While official death tolls are unknown, some estimations go as high as two hundred million lives lost.

This book will cover what is known about the origins of the Black Death, as well as how it spread across several continents. We will then talk about how the Black Death still affects us today and how the world has adapted to it. Because, yes, this deadly disease is still out there! But keep reading because there's some good news along with all the bad.

Join us then as we journey back over seven hundred years ago to a period full of danger and a fight for survival. Discover the enduring human spirit in the most trying of times. It will not be an easy historical period to examine, but it will be well worth it!

Chapter 1: Origins and Spread of the Black Death

Though understanding about the Black Death was limited at the time of its spread, it is now understood that it was caused by a bacterium (singular form of bacteria) known as *Yersinia pestis* (*Y. pestis*). While the Black Death ravaged Europe in the mid-1300s, it wasn't until 1894 that the specific bacterium that caused the plague was discovered by a physician and bacteriologist by the name of Alexandre Yersin. Originally, the bacterium was known as *Pasteurella pestis* and eventually was renamed after Yersin after his death. While many of you might not be eager to have a deadly bacterium named after you, for many scientists, this is an immense honor!

There was another scientist hard at work to uncover the source of the Black Death at almost the exact same time as Yersin. This researcher was Kitasato Shibasaburo, a Japanese bacteriologist. While Kitasato uncovered the origins, Yersin often gets the credit, as his report was more comprehensive. However, some academics give both men credit for the discovery. Because of their hard work, we are able to understand how this deadly disease is spread.

Y. pestis is a rod-shaped bacterium. When a virus enters our bodies, the first thing our immune system does is send our defense cells, also known as macrophages, to get rid of the intruder. However, the toxins in *Y. pestis* are so aggressive that it does not take long before our defense cells are defeated, allowing the bacterium to multiply with abandon.

Now, before we get into how the Black Death can pass so quickly between people, let's dive into a few of the terms that you will see a lot of in this book.

The two most common are the Black Death and the bubonic plague or, for our purposes, just plague. These both refer to the same disease, but bubonic plague is a bit more scientific. While we'll get further into detail on the specific symptoms in the next chapter, what you need to know is that bubonic refers to swollen lymph nodes. These are most commonly found in the neck, armpit, and groin areas.

A plague refers to a bacterial disease with severe symptoms, such as fever and a chest infection. There are three types of plague: bubonic, septicemic, and pneumonic. In this case, the Black Death generally began as a bubonic plague that then morphed into one or both of the other types of plague.

The term Black Death started being used after observing the way many peoples' skins turned black as their infection worsened.

Black Death and bubonic plague will both be used over the course of this book. Other names that have been used through time include the Blue Sickness, the Pestilence, and the Great Mortality. We likely won't use any of those names, but it's always interesting to see how names change over time.

While many people quote rats as the spreader of this violent disease, after much study, it was determined that something even smaller was to blame: fleas. These tiny creatures became infected with *Y. pestis* and would go on to infect bigger creatures, such as rats, mice, squirrels, and rabbits, through bites. But how would the virus then pass on to humans?

Unfortunately, bubonic plague is incredibly contagious and can spread in almost every way imaginable. Before a virus passes from an animal to a human, there is typically something that happens called an epizootic. An epizootic is basically an outbreak of a disease similar to a pandemic or epidemic for humans, except it's happening within an animal population. An example of an epizootic is bovine spongiform encephalopathy, more commonly known as mad cow disease. Almost 200,000 cows have died of the disease, along with 150 people.

In the case of mad cow disease, the humans who contracted it did so through eating meat from an infected cow, but there are many other ways for viruses to spread.

In the case of the Black Death, once smaller animals died, many fleas infected with the plague searched for bigger prey. Because rats are so common in bigger cities, it was natural for humans to be the next choice. However, it wasn't just flea bites that could pass on the disease. Because the virus is present in blood and other bodily fluids, many people caught it simply from handling diseased animals. For example, someone might have prepared and eaten a diseased animal before it was showing symptoms. Or a beloved pet might have killed a rodent and then passed the disease onto its owner. It might seem obvious to stay away from someone who is clearly sick, but by the time symptoms were present, it might have been too late. Besides, many people at the time had no idea how the virus was spreading, so it's understandable why proper precautions weren't always taken.

The exact origins of the Black Death aren't known, but it is generally agreed that it originated somewhere in central Asia. In the mid- to late 1330s, there was a settlement near Issyk-Kul Lake, which is a mountain lake that is now part of modern-day Kyrgyzstan. The settlement was full of traders, a profession that you will soon understand had a key role in the rapid spread of the disease.

1346 1347 1348 1349 1350 1351 1352 1353

- - - Approximate border between the Principality of Kiev and the Golden Horde - passage prohibited for Christians.

Land trade routes

Maritime trade routes

A map of how the disease spread from 1346 to 1353.

How and where the disease spread for the next several years is unknown, but it eventually made its way to Feodosiya, then known as Kaffa, which lies on the Crimean Peninsula in Ukraine. It is generally thought that it was brought there by Mongolian traders.

Wherever it originated from, what we do know for sure is that it was able to spread so quickly because of the trading routes that stretched across Asia and Europe. While it has not been confirmed, it has been suggested that Mongolian warriors catapulted infected bodies into the town of Feodosiya in an attempt to bring down their enemies. Quite a vivid image if it happened!

However, even without catapulting bodies, the Black Death still paints horrific images to think about now. From Feodosiya, several ships set sail for Mediterranean ports. At this period in time, the Silk Road was at the height of its operation. Trading routes crisscrossed their way across Asia, Europe, and North Africa, covering around four thousand miles of land and sea. It's not hard to imagine how a network of paths like this might spread a deadly disease.

In 1347, several ships pulled into the port of Sicily. There were other ports that plague ships pulled into around this time, including ports in France, Spain, Britain, and Ireland, but Sicily is one of the most well-documented cases. What Sicilians discovered when they boarded the ships was horrifying.

Many of the sailors were already dead, and those who were still alive were very ill. It was immediately decided that the ships should be sent back out to sea, but unfortunately, it was already too late. The Black Death had arrived in Sicily, and it soon began to spread inland.

As we'll discuss in the next chapter, the incubation period for the Black Death can be lengthy, so many people were contagious for several days without even knowing it. Because of this, people traveled along roads and into different ports, spreading it to dozens of people, who then went on to infect hundreds of cities with incredible speed. And, of course, communication between different areas at this time was slow, so sometimes by the time a neighboring city caught wind of the fact that the infection was spreading nearby, it had already arrived in their community.

The Black Death continued to decimate populations until 1352 when the worst of the first wave began to decline. This by no means signaled the eradication of the disease, but fatality levels certainly decreased until the second wave during the 1500s.

Of course, there were attempts to limit the spread of the virus, with varying success rates. One of the most common safety measures at the time is a precaution that is still used during outbreaks experienced today: quarantines.

A quarantine is when an individual, a population, or an entire ship is put under lockdown with strict instructions not to leave their designated area. This is done in the hopes that the contagion won't be able to escape the confines of the quarantine, therefore keeping the surrounding community members safe.

It became standard practice to quarantine all ships coming into European harbors for thirty days and then, later, forty days. The Italian word for forty days is *quaranta giorni*, which is where the word quarantine comes from. Why the time period of forty days was chosen is not known exactly, but there are a few theories.

In religious texts, the Great Flood lasted for forty days, Moses fasted for forty days, and after Jesus was resurrected, he spent forty days with his disciples. Forty days could have also had something to do with Hippocrates's theory of illness or even the Pythagorean theory of numbers.

Regardless of why it was chosen, forty days became the standard period of time for sailors to be quarantined in the hope of limiting the spread of the disease.

Populations also learned to be very careful of products that arrived on these boats as well. Fabric, in particular, was suspected to be one of the worst transmitters and would be vigorously washed and aired out for two days before being handled.

During the Black Death, measures now known as social distancing began to be employed. When new ships entered Italian harbors, captains would speak with safety officers through a window in a separate room.

Of course, these measures were implemented differently (it was a different place and time), and many of them were based on guesswork as to how the virus spread. The hypotheses were not always correct.

During this time, plague doctors were a common sight in cities. These doctors would visit people who had a suspected infection and prescribe a quarantine or other safety measure if they were ill. They could also be used as witnesses on wills, which exploded in popularity during this time. These doctors handed out a variety of different medicines, none of which proved to be at all effective. While the disease can be treated with a course of antibiotics today, at the time, no such treatment was available. Instead, doctors would attempt to cure the illness by using rose water on victims or using the popular practice of bloodletting. Bloodletting, which could be done either manually or through the use of leeches, was thought to rid the body of impurities and balance the "humors" within a person's bodily fluids. It is now understood that bloodletting does no such thing.

Stranger than bloodletting was the outfit that later plague doctors wore. Although these outfits didn't actually come into vogue until the 16th and 17th centuries, they are so closely associated with the Black Death that they deserve a mention.

An image of a plague doctor.
https://commons.wikimedia.org/wiki/File:Paul_F%C3%BCrst,_Der_Doctor_Schnabel_von_Rom_(coloured_version).png

The outfit consisted of long pants that connected to large boots. A shirt would be tucked into the pants, and a coat with a protective coating of scented wax would be worn. Plague doctors also had a hat and gloves that were typically constructed out of goat leather, as well as a cane they could use to poke suspected plague victims.

However, the most astonishing feature of this uniform was the mask. Not only did plague doctors put on glasses, but they also wore large birdlike masks that gave them a sinister appearance. The long beaks featured two small holes for breathing.

While it is now known that the plague can spread through droplets transmitted through the air, at the time, most doctors believed that it was due to the aforementioned imbalance of humors. Therefore, it was thought that the right concoction of flowers and herbs could prevent the spread of the disease into the nostrils. Because of this, doctors would fill their masks with herbs and perfumes, falsely believing that the scent would prevent the inhalation of poisoned air.

While the addition of perfume and open breathing holes clearly didn't prevent the spread of disease, there was some wisdom in the original design of this outfit. Medical professionals working with infectious diseases often do so in disposable medical garb that doesn't allow for any skin or orifice to be exposed to outside air. In some cases, full hazmat suits might even be worn. Of course, we now know that face masks that completely cover the mouth and nose are one of the most effective tools we have against airborne viruses, so perhaps it would be pleasing to some of the plague doctors from the past to know that their outfit design wasn't totally pointless.

Vicary Method

One rather bizarre method used to attempt to cure the Black Death was something invented by a man named Thomas Vicary, and it's certainly not for the faint of heart. Although introduced during a later outbreak of the bubonic plague in the 16th century, this method is indicative of the lengths people went to in order to combat this deadly disease. The Vicary Method was employed by plucking all the feathers off of a chicken's backside. That's right; a bare chicken's bum was an essential part of this so-called cure. The bare chicken bottom would then be strapped onto one of the boils on a patient's body. Oh, and it's important to mention that this would all be done while the chicken was still alive!

The idea was that the chicken would breathe in the infection through their bottom because, at the time, it was believed that chickens breathed through that area of their bodies. It might seem ridiculous now, but when you think about the fact that these people were dealing with a disease that was killing millions at a rapid rate, you can't really blame them for trying anything they thought might help.

Once the chicken got sick, it would be removed, cleaned, and then reattached. Obviously, this method didn't succeed in doing anything other than humiliating and infecting a chicken!

Another attempt to curb the spread was the use of plague hospitals. These hospitals sprang up all over Europe and were used as isolation centers for the sick. While not all of these hospitals were pleasant, for many, it was an attempt to allow dignity to those in their final stretch of life while simultaneously protecting the lives of the community members around them.

Unfortunately, attempts to limit the spread were not particularly successful. This was partly due to the limited understanding of how the disease spread but also because it was hard to enforce some of the restrictions. People would flee quarantined areas in the hope of escaping the virus, only to unknowingly take it to another community.

Several cities began implementing death penalties for anyone who tried to cross in or out of a quarantine zone without permission. Traders were looked down on with particular disdain and were often forbidden from entering cities on their trade routes.

Antisemitism and the Black Death

Antisemitism was already rampant throughout Christian communities in Europe for decades before the Black Death took hold. There had been many cases of Jewish communities being murdered across the continent. However, there are some accounts that recall how Jewish communities were falsely accused of having been the ones responsible for the plague outbreak. This completely unsubstantiated claim resulted in massacres of Jewish communities in areas like Germany and Spain. While historians differ on the exact details, pandemics often see certain communities face horrific persecution. If someone wants to attack a specific group, they need very little fuel for their fire.

While there have been several pandemics throughout history, none have been as damaging as the Black Death, and that is in large part due to the speed at which it spread. It is estimated that the virus covered anywhere from 1.5 to 6 kilometers (less than a mile to almost 4 miles) a day. This is even more incredible when you consider the limited speed of transportation in those days.

By the end of the first wave of the plague, it had wiped out almost a third and possibly even up to two-thirds of Europe's population. In some cities, almost 90 percent of the citizens died. The elderly and the immunocompromised were particularly vulnerable to the virus's attack.

The survivors of the first round of the plague might provide a clue as to why the outcomes of the next waves weren't as severe. Although the Black Death continued to see waves for the next five hundred years, the death counts generally weren't as high. This is possibly due to the fact that the ancestors of the next group of people affected by the pandemic were the ones who were able to survive the first wave. This chilling display of natural selection perhaps passed down the ability to be able to withstand the virus, which might explain the lower death counts in the years that followed.

However, even with this slight advantage, the death tolls from the Black Death were staggering. During the summer of 1665, the plague took hold in London, England. During May, only forty-three people died, but by the end of the summer, the virus had killed 15 percent of the city's population. If that level of devastation was possible in just one city during a less severe wave of the pandemic, you can imagine how bad it must have been overall. In fact, after the first wave, it took almost two hundred years for western Europe to reach the same population level that it had had prior to the pandemic.

An illustration of the plague in London in 1665.
https://commons.wikimedia.org/wiki/File:Great_plague_of_london-1665.jpg

Chapter 2: Symptoms and Progression

The incubation period for the bubonic plague is generally four to seven days. However, symptoms can present in as little as twenty-four hours after exposure and can also sometimes wait to present after the week mark. This unpredictable time period would have made it very difficult for people to know who was infected.

During the incubation phase, *Y. pestis* attacks the immune system, but the body is attempting to put up a defense, so there are no obvious signs of the disease at this stage.

One of the most frightening aspects of the plague is how quickly symptoms can appear. Someone might appear to be in perfectly good health and then the next moment be deathly ill.

Fever

People experiencing the Black Death often came down with an extremely high fever that seemed to come out of nowhere. Fevers were often accompanied by severe chills that were almost impossible to manage.

Fatigue

The sudden onset of extreme fatigue was another indicator that the Black Death might be on its way. In the mid-1300s, many people worked as laborers and were used to long, strenuous days. However, the overwhelming tiredness that hit them as a result of the plague left them unable to leave their beds.

Weakness

The plague had the power to take someone from Olympian-level strength to a wave of exhaustion from simply lifting a finger.

Headache

A pounding headache would often overwhelm victims of the plague.

Light Sensitivity

People infected with the Black Death often complained about the harshness of light.

Unusual Tongue Appearance

People who were developing bubonic plague symptoms often had a white or swollen tongue just before their lymph nodes began to swell.

Muscle Aches

While nobody who contracted the plague was in any position to do any exercise, their entire body felt like they had just been put through the most punishing workout imaginable.

Swollen Lymph Nodes

The most distinguishing feature of the Black Death was swollen lymph nodes. Lymph nodes are filters that run throughout our bodies to help drain waste products from our system. They also contain cells called lymphocytes that can destroy harmful bacteria. When our lymph nodes are trying to fight off an infection, they often become swollen. When swollen, the lymph node is referred to as a bubo, which is how the bubonic plague gets its name.

We have lymph nodes in various areas of our bodies, but the areas that are most visible to produce lumps are our neck, armpits, and groin. Not only will these buboes swell to an uncomfortable size, but they can also swell to the point where they need to release some pressure and can actually start to leak pus and sometimes even blood.

These are often the first symptoms that people infected with the Black Death experienced, but each infection was different. Some people would immediately exhibit more serious symptoms. Because no treatments existed at the time, almost everyone ended up exhibiting those symptoms eventually.

There are three different types of plague. While we mainly use the term bubonic plague in this book, the other types, septicemic and pneumonic, can and often do result from an initial bubonic infection. Most of the time, if one does not receive treatment, that is exactly what would happen.

Septicemic plague is the reason why this pandemic was so often referred to as the Black Death. When a patient reached this stage, it was because the *Y. pestis* had multiplied to such an extent that it was beginning to completely take over the body.

Patients with septicemic plague might have started in the bubonic phase or skipped immediately to this much more serious version of the plague. At this stage, the body begins to shut down, which results in gangrene, which stops the normal flow of blood in your body, particularly to areas like your fingers and toes. This kills off skin and tissue, resulting in a black, almost charred look that presents in patches. Once blood flow has been disrupted and the tissue has died, there is no reviving it. While modern medicine can prevent septicemic plague from progressing, without it, the infection will likely kill you within forty-eight hours. The only way to stop the spread without treatment is by amputating the infected areas.

As if that wasn't bad enough, this stage usually comes with severe gastrointestinal symptoms, including nausea, violent vomiting, and diarrhea.

Following the fever you get in the initial stages of septicemic plague, your body will go into a stage known as sepsis. While dead and blackened tissue is the external evidence of this condition, something even worse is happening on the inside. Your body is working so hard to fight off the attack that it creates an internal inflammatory response. This doesn't just disrupt blood flow to the skin; it also affects the blood flow to all your other organs, like your kidney, your heart, and your brain. Even in modern times, sepsis can easily be fatal or cause lifelong medical issues. During the Middle Ages, no treatment was available, so the mortality rate was very high.

Septicemic plague is an incredibly serious condition that can frequently have fatal outcomes, but there was another stage that patients could enter known as pneumonic plague. This, maybe shockingly, is the deadliest form of the disease and is the stage where the virus can be spread via droplets. Pneumonic plague is when the virus has spread to the lungs. While all stages of the plague can include the initial symptoms we listed, the following symptoms are more specific to pneumonic plague.

Breathing Issues

People often reported having shortness of breath and a feeling like they couldn't get enough air into their lungs.

Chest Pain

Because blood flow was restricted, the heart had to work harder than it should, which could result in sharp or constant pain in the chest area.

Coughing

The lungs began to fill with fluid, which made it difficult to breathe and also resulted in consistent coughing. This coughing would be loud and painful and could often produce blood or thick mucus.

Delirium

Because the virus took such a terrific toll on the body, many people would end up in a delirious state. It is said that some would end up babbling incoherently in their final moments on earth.

Even if someone didn't immediately have the pneumonic plague, it was generally just a matter of time before they got there—that is if one of the other two stages didn't end their life first. Without treatment, an infected person could go from being seemingly fine to dead in just a matter of days. It was a quick and devastating disease.

Because the onset of symptoms was so quick and the treatments were far from perfect, the Black Death made its way through populations like wildfire. City officials were soon overwhelmed by bodies and began to dispose of victims of the plague in mass graves. Many people who were charged with handling the victims went on to contract the disease themselves.

An 18th-century mass grave filled with plague victims.
https://commons.wikimedia.org/wiki/File:Bubonic_plague_victims-mass_grave_in_Martigues,_France_1720-1721.jpg

The deaths might have been quick, but they were far from painless. The disease quickly took over every area of the body, leaving victims writhing in agony. Because so little was known about the spread and out of a desperate attempt to stop the pandemic from getting worse, many faced the end of their lives alone or stuffed into crowded rooms filled with other sick members of the population.

The plague continued to ravage Asia, North Africa, and Europe until 1352 when it began to diminish. Though it didn't completely disappear, it was quiet enough that many people were able to go about their normal lives without too much fear. However, less than a decade later, it came back for another wave, which lasted for two more years. By 1363, it had died down again, but it came back just a few years later in 1369. You can probably see a pattern emerging here.

The Black Death continued to visit the citizens of the world on and off over the ensuing decades. However, the second large wave didn't happen until the 1500s, when a new strain attacked with renewed vigor. The final big wave of the disease happened in the 1800s. While it is still possible to contract the Black Death today, the final wave saw some major scientific advancements that rendered it relatively harmless if caught quickly enough.

Chapter 3: Medieval Medicinal Struggles

As mentioned earlier, doctors and the general public at the time had interesting ideas about how to treat infectious diseases. But of course, they didn't have access to fancy labs with advanced microscopes and the scientific know-how that we have today. For example, we now accept the germ theory, the idea that specific organisms are responsible for specific diseases. However, during the 1300s, there was no real concept of what germs were or how a disease could be passed from person to person. Instead, the general public believed in something called miasma theory.

Where exactly the miasma theory comes from is unknown, but it was a theory upheld by a Greek physician named Hippocrates. During the first two waves of the Black Death, the idea took hold of communities all over Europe.

The idea behind the miasma theory was that air that smelled foul was the sign of a poisonous substance present. If this poisonous air was breathed in, it could infect the breather. This was why doctors eventually wore the long beak-like masks filled with various perfumes and flowers. They were trying to keep the miasma out! Bacteria wasn't understood, so it was just believed that bad air, in general, was evil and to be avoided if at all possible.

Interestingly, although the miasma theory wasn't exactly correct, it did help facilitate some changes that ended up having a positive impact on health and safety around the world. Because of the miasma theory, sewage and sanitation measures started being implemented in cities and towns. Proper sanitation is a crucial element of a healthy society, but it was implemented for the wrong reasons because of the miasma theory.

In the case of the bubonic plague, many victims of the disease were said to have an unpleasant odor, which was believed to be a dangerous element to others. However, it's unsurprising that anyone in the final stages of the plague would have a bad smell. Their organs were shutting down. They were vomiting and coughing up blood, and they had boils all over their bodies that were oozing pus and blood. The inevitable smell was likely shocking to the nose, but it had nothing to do with spreading the virus.

Similarly, during periods when raw sewage was left in the street, many people got sick due to the contamination of their drinking supply and any accidental contact people had with waste. The smell, while unpleasant, didn't have anything to do with the disease outbreaks.

So, even though incorrect conclusions were drawn about the miasma theory, it did help change some areas of society for the better. Sadly, however, perfume did not stop anyone from contracting the bubonic plague.

Interestingly, there was another concept that was held in high regard during this time period, and it can also be traced back to Greek physicians, including Hippocrates and Galen. The basic concept of the four humors, or humor theory, is the idea that the body contains four different liquids: black bile, yellow bile, blood, and phlegm. The theory was that in order to prevent sickness, a person needed to keep all of these liquids balanced within their body.

Each of the four humors was connected to a particular condition, and there were different requirements for how much of each humor should be present in a person's body. It was also thought that men and women required a different balance.

The belief in the theory of the humors was so strong that during the Renaissance, there was even a specific diet one could follow in an attempt to balance their humors. What was particularly fascinating about humor theory was that the people who believed in it did not recognize diseases as an attack on the body that was coming from an outside source. Instead, it was assumed that any kind of ailment was simply due to an imbalance that could be rectified with some kind of treatment. Because of this, a variety of aggressive purging methods were used. Let's dive into the specifics of the four humors and what was done in an attempt to balance one's body.

Blood

Blood was generally considered the most important humor, which, all things considered, was a fairly good assessment. People who were considered to have an excess of blood were said to have a sanguine temperament. The definition of sanguine is someone who is generally optimistic, especially in dire circumstances. Not a bad quality to have when facing the prospect of a brutal death!

Excess blood was most commonly associated with springtime and was thought to be connected to qualities of wetness and heat.

While humor theory has long ago been debunked, there is still a persistence in thinking that our bodies have these four different temperaments. Because of this, there are specific suggestions for each temperament group. For sanguine or more blood-heavy people, the recommendation is to stay away from heavy foods, such as red meat and too much bread. Instead, it is suggested they eat light, summery foods, as well as lots of vegetables.

Bloodletting, as mentioned earlier, was a popular treatment for many ailments at this time, but it was seen as particularly useful for anyone suspected of having too much blood. There were a variety of ways to draw blood depending on one's preference or, more commonly, one's social class.

Leeching: If you're already squeamish, that's not surprising. Leeching is pretty much exactly what it sounds like. Doctors would apply live leeches to a patient's body and allow them to suck blood from the patient (or, perhaps more appropriately, victim) until it was determined that they had removed enough to balance the humors. Because bloodletting remained popular for so long, owning and distributing leeches became a lucrative profession. It could sometimes be difficult to procure leeches for a reasonable price, so this type of bloodletting was generally reserved for the wealthy. A fun, or perhaps disgusting, fact is that leeches can drink several times their own body weight in blood. Some of them are able to consume up to ten milliliters at a time.

Cupping: Not as common at the time was cupping. Small incisions would be made into the skin, often by several small blades. Then, a small cup would be heated and suctioned onto the skin in an attempt to draw disease away from the body. This was often done directly on top of buboes since they were the most obvious symptoms of illness. Anyone who has received cupping today can probably imagine how uncomfortable that must have been to receive!

Venesection: For those who weren't able to afford leeches, bloodletting by incision was usually the most common method. This involved a small cut made by a thumb lancet or a fleam. A lancet is a small, double-sided blade. A fleam typically had several blades of different sizes, kind of like the blade you might take with you on a camping trip. After the incision was completed, the blood would be collected under the incision point with a dish. The incision would often be made on a vein very close to the crease of the elbow, but that wasn't always the case.

Because so many people fell sick during this period of time and since the general understanding of disease was so limited, the physicians in charge of administering these treatments were incredibly inconsistent. In many cases, they might not have even been physicians at all. Therefore, the amount of blood withdrawn could vary greatly, sometimes leaving the patient incredibly weak and faint.

Yellow Bile

Yellow bile was thought to signify a choleric temperament. This meant someone who was particularly ambitious and aggressive, often lacking in patience. It was closely associated with the summer season.

Interestingly, bloodletting was not only a solution for what was perceived as an excess of blood but also an excess of all the humors in general. It was almost seen as a magic cure-all. This is fascinating since all bloodletting really did was weaken the person who was on the receiving end of it.

There were a variety of other "treatments" used in an attempt to cure the plague and balance the humors, but since they were often used for any perceived imbalances, we'll cover them after talking about the next two humors.

Black Bile

Black bile was thought to be in excess when someone had a melancholy personality. However, it seems difficult to imagine that anyone who was suffering from the bubonic plague would be anything other than melancholy.

Black bile was thought to mean a person had an excess of dryness and coldness within them and was most closely associated with autumn, although sometimes people would associate it with winter instead. It was suggested that a person with a melancholy personality eat more warm, cooked foods and anything that might have a natural laxative effect.

Phlegm

Although the thought of phlegm might not conjure up any appetizing images, someone with a phlegmatic personality type was seen as a person who was actually quite solid and consistent. They were perceived to be hardworking and quick to take accountability. However, that quality was sometimes to their detriment.

Phlegmatic personalities are generally associated with winter, and people with an excess of phlegm are thought to have a lot of moisture and coldness in their bodies. It was suggested that phlegmatics eat flavorful and salty diets with lots of garlic and onions. A popular method for trying to rid people of excess phlegm was to encourage them to vomit.

Speaking of vomit, now that we have covered the prevailing theories of the time, let's go into more detail about some of the outrageous and sometimes frankly disgusting treatments provided to patients. One of the more bizarre treatments happened during one of the later waves of the plague in the 1660s.

Although Isaac Newton is famous for uncovering the laws of motion and light that are still accepted today, it is perhaps reassuring to know that even geniuses have some very bad ideas.

In 2020, a few of Newton's personal notes were sold at auction, and one of them presented an unusual cure for the bubonic plague. Here is what the note said:

"The best is a toad suspended by the legs in a chimney for three days, which at last vomited up earth with various insects in it, on to a dish of yellow wax, and shortly after died. Combining powdered toad with the excretions and serum made into lozenges and worn about the affected area drove away the contagion and drew out the poison."

Interestingly, this lozenge wasn't the only toad remedy that was recommended to help combat the plague! During this same time period, many people took to wearing dried toads around their necks. This was done not because anyone thought toads were a nice fashion accessory but because they believed that the toxins from the toad would help to draw out toxins from the body. As you can probably guess, the toads did no such thing.

However, toads aren't the only remedies people have tried. Let's dive into some of the other interesting attempts people made at ridding their bodies of the Black Death.

1. Vinegar

Vinegar became quite popular during the Black Death and was often used in an attempt to ward off the disease. A popular story circulated that four thieves entered a residence to loot it after its inhabitants died of the plague, but the thieves somehow never got sick themselves. It was said they covered themselves with a vinegar tonic before they entered the home and were able to keep themselves healthy by doing so.

There were several different versions of the four thieves' vinegar tonic, and it is highly likely that each person who made it used a slightly different variation based on what they had on hand. Although the tonic isn't a cure for the plague, there are still some who are curious about the ingredients and make it because they believe it will be of use to them in some way (those who use it today believe it wards off the common cold; no scientific studies have been conducted to prove this).

The following are some of the most common herbs and ingredients you might find. Although the exact benefits of the ingredients weren't known at the time, many of them do, in fact, have some beneficial medicinal qualities.

Cloves – Cloves have a strong and pleasant scent and some antimicrobial benefits.

Garlic – Anyone who has ever experienced a common cold has probably received the advice to eat some garlic. It has been used in medicine for thousands of years and was often added to the four thieves' tonic.

Sage – It helps with inflammation and has antibacterial properties.

Thyme – It might help combat some infections and is rich in antioxidants.

Cinnamon – Another lovely scent, cinnamon has antioxidant and antifungal benefits.

In the book *Aromatherapy*, the French chemist Jean Gattefossé presented a recipe for the tonic:

"Take three pints of strong white wine vinegar, add a handful of each of wormwood, meadowsweet, wild marjoram and sage, fifty cloves, two ounces of campanula roots, two ounces of angelic, rosemary and horehound and three large measures of champhor. Place the mixture in a container for fifteen days, strain and express then bottle. Use by rubbing it on the hands, ears and temples from time to time when approaching a plague victim."

2. Snakes

If you thought the plague treatments ended with chickens, leeches, and toads, then think again! Snakes had been used in some medical treatments prior to the Black Death, so the idea of using them wasn't exactly new. However, how they were used in this context was likely upsetting for the poor people on the receiving end.

At the time, snakes were often seen as evil creatures. They were sneaky and moved in an unusual way, and many of them were poisonous. Because of this, it was thought that the wickedness of the snake could draw out the wickedness of the plague. So, physicians would chop snakes up into pieces and lay them over the patient's buboes. Not exactly a comforting thing to have happen to you when you are moments away from death.

3. Urine Baths and Feces Paste

It turns out there were treatments that were even worse than chopped-up snakes or a raw chicken bum. At the time, it was believed that urine had powerful medicinal properties, and people would sometimes bathe in it and even drink it in the hopes of benefiting from the golden potion.

Scientists have since proven that urine holds no medicinal benefits, at least none that you can't find from a better source. Even so, the rumor that urine is sterile is still a myth that persists today. However, at the time, the demand for urine was sometimes quite high. Just like with leech breeding, sourcing "good" urine was a rather profitable profession for a period during the Middle Ages.

Now, if for some strange reason you didn't want to dunk yourself into a bath of pee, there was another option available to you: a paste made out of human excrement.

Similar to the snake theory, human feces would be rubbed onto a person's boils with the idea that it would draw the illness out. It hardly needs to be said that not only would that not work, but it would also very likely make the person die faster. Plus, it would have smelled disgusting.

But again, these were people living in desperate times, so it's understandable that they would have been willing to try anything they thought might help them get better.

4. Onions

After chopped-up snakes and feces, the idea of rubbing onions all over your body might not sound too bad!

Onions were generally used in a similar way to the last few methods, as they would be rubbed against the signature boils produced when experiencing the bubonic plague. Not only was it believed that onions would help draw out the toxins, but it was also thought that onions were a powerful combatant to miasma, which we covered earlier.

5. Unicorns

That's right, it was thought that unicorns were capable of curing the plague. You might be understandably confused, and so were people in the medieval period.

We know that unicorns don't actually exist, so instead, the horns that were used were sourced from narwhals or occasionally from rhinos. Once the horn was collected, it was ground into a powder and mixed with water to be consumed. Of course, this concoction was only available to the very wealthy since unicorns were notoriously hard to capture. Some said they could only be caught by a virgin woman. It seems highly unlikely that any narwals or rhinos were captured by young virgins, but then again, people thought they were drinking the horn of a real unicorn, so they likely believed the story.

6. Flagellation

As has already been stated, there were many who believed the Black Death to be something wicked and evil. And so, it makes sense that many took the plague to be a punishment from God for their sins. In the hopes of paying for their sins, groups of people took to the streets and publicly whipped themselves, often with whips embedded with nails.

Of course, this did nothing except wound people who were likely already sick.

7. Expensive Powder

"Unicorn" powder wasn't the only expensive substance that was mixed into water for people to drink. Another popular potion was the beautiful shiny gem made famous in *The Wonderful Wizard of Oz*: emeralds. Doctors would crush emeralds into a powder and have their patients eat or drink it. Why this was seen as a possible cure is unclear, but then again, that question could be asked about many of the items on this list.

8. Cheap Powders

Of course, the previously listed powders came at a cost and were only available to those who could pay. But it seems that the idea of drinking a powdered drink took hold of the general population, so cheaper and more easily accessible ingredients were substituted for those who weren't able to afford a gem or mythical animal. Both have a long history of being used for various medical conditions, but the reality is that neither of them plays any role in healing a person and could have the opposite effect. Both arsenic and mercury are incredibly toxic and can kill very fast upon consumption. Why they continued to be used after so many people died soon after drinking these potions is a confusing question that has no answer.

9. Theriac

Theriac was a very popular concoction during the Black Death. It was a highly intricate recipe that required dozens of ingredients. It could be used as a paste spread over the skin or was sometimes mixed with a thinner liquid and drunk as a beverage. When made into liquid, it was sometimes called treacle.

While theriac contained many ingredients, including the alarming addition of viper flesh, there is one ingredient in particular that might help to explain its popularity: opium. Opium is a well-known painkiller, and this substance often contained high levels of the drug within its recipe.

Theriac wasn't just a product of the plague; it had also been used by different cultures for centuries, dating all the way back to Mithridates VI, who was alive during the 3rd century BCE.

Out of all the supposed treatments for the Black Death, this is one of the only ones that seemed to provide any actual benefit. However, it is thought that most of that benefit was actually due to the placebo effect. While theriac is still talked about today, there haven't been many studies done on the original recipes, so it's hard to know if it could have helped. However, if nothing else, it probably helped to relieve the pain suffered by plague victims, and it certainly must have smelled better than onions or feces!

10. Fire

Another method people used to try to rid themselves of disease was to sit beside extremely hot fires. It was believed that a person could sweat out a disease if they stayed by a fire long enough or that the heat would destroy infected air. While the thinking behind this wasn't completely accurate, there was definite value to the idea of combating the plague with heat. We'll get to that in more detail in a later chapter.

One particular proponent of the heat method was Pope Clement VI, who was the head of the Catholic Church when the first wave of the plague hit. On the advice of his physicians, the pope spent most of his days in a large room with a roaring fire at either end. He also kept to himself, essentially quarantining inside a room of fire.

For the pope, at least, this method worked, and he died from unrelated causes in 1352.

11. Air

As we talked about earlier, there was a strong belief in the idea of miasma, and many people tried to use that theory to their advantage. It was common to attempt to cleanse the air in one's home by using various herbs and perfumes. Some people would even carry flowers around with them at all times, believing that they wouldn't contract the plague if they were constantly breathing in a pleasant aroma.

Others had the opposite belief and thought that staying near rancid smells would help to draw disease away from them. Because of this, they might stand next to sewage or even decomposing remains, believing that the plague would be overwhelmingly attracted to the bad air and leave their bodies to seek out miasma instead.

12. Quarantine

The only effective method of preventing the spread of the Black Death at the time was quarantining. This obviously did nothing to help people already infected with it, but separating the sick from the healthy did help limit the spread.

Social distancing was another proven method of prevention. However, both quarantining and social distancing were met with disdain by many. It was common to have people purposefully disobey quarantine orders and either move from cities or visit those who were already known to be sick. This resulted in many more people falling ill than if they had followed quarantine and social distancing recommendations.

This disregard for public safety measures has been repeated throughout history. This has often led to extremely strict and sometimes violent lockdowns by local governments. Still, scientists emphasize that quarantining is a very effective and useful measure until the disease in question is under control.

There were undoubtedly countless other treatments used over the years as the Black Death made its way around the world. But these were the ones that were popular enough to still have records of them preserved today. Thankfully, we are much more knowledgeable in modern times, so no one has to strap a chicken to themselves anymore!

Chapter 4: Europe during the Plague

Although the Black Death was present on several continents, it greatly impacted Europe. After its arrival in the 1330s, waves of the disease continued to roll through the continent for hundreds of years, killing millions and leaving many cities altered for generations. Let's look at some of the most dramatic changes that happened during this time.

Conflict

The Black Death had an interesting impact on conflict. Initially, it was so overwhelming that it caused a pause in the conflicts of the day, but that soon reversed in a dramatic fashion, resulting in even more violence than had been experienced previously. During the Hundred Years' War, fighting had to stop completely for a time, as the military was overrun with deaths.

Labor

One of the biggest issues to come out of the Black Death was the loss of workers. One of the most common professions at the time was laborers who worked in agriculture. This was before modern technology greatly reduced the need for physical bodies to tend the land, and workers at the time were an essential element for the production of food and the cultivation of land and animals.

With such significant death tolls, landowners suddenly found themselves without anyone to tend to their farms, and they quickly began to panic. But this was where a small silver lining of the Black Death appeared.

Before the arrival of the bubonic plague, field laborers were seen as some of the lowest members of society. They were peasants who were paid extremely poor wages and were often only making enough to get by. However, the plague changed everything.

Because so many workers died, the landowners no longer had the upper hand, and menial workers could now demand more. With no other choice, they had to provide their workers with good wages or risk losing their profits entirely. The loss of lives also reduced the cost of land, and suddenly, rents cost next to nothing.

This greatly reduced the number of people in the peasant class and gave many people who had survived the plague a better quality of life. And not only did landowners finally have to pay their workers a reasonable wage, but many of them had to actually go to work themselves! While they had previously looked down on many of the jobs on their land, they could no longer afford to be particular. They, too, had to get out in the dirt and get their hands dirty.

However, this idyllic moment of equality was short-lived. Not satisfied with simply paying their employees a living wage, landowners quickly turned to the law to deal with their issues. This issue was particularly fraught in England, where the imposed laws eventually led to a revolt.

In England, a statute was pushed through that followed the details of an ordinance that was passed in 1349. The ordinance stated that anyone under the age of sixty who was not able to work privately was required to work. Not only were they required to work, but they also had to sign contracts that agreed to only pay them wages that had been established prior to the appearance of the Black Death. This meant a swift return to the poverty wages that had been so common prior to the pandemic. It's also important to consider that not only were these wages poor, but they were also being forced upon people who were very likely performing much more work than had previously been required of them. Laborers always had strenuous jobs, but with the loss of so many lives, they had to pick up the slack somehow and were still expected to do so for very low pay.

And it wasn't as though workers could simply refuse to take the work. The ordinance required that they take the first job offered to them, and they could be severely punished if they refused and remained unemployed. This forced workers into a very tight corner and gave power back to the landowners.

This is a common theme during pandemics. A worker shortage happens, and bosses reluctantly pay their workers more, as it is suddenly acknowledged that these so-called "lowly" workers are actually essential. However, once the panic wears off, the people in charge do everything they can to claw back any benefits they give their workers in the hopes of maximizing profits and lining their own pockets.

However, in the case of the Black Death, the renewed power of the landowners didn't last long. The measures lasted for several years, but resentment continued to brew. Under King Richard II, tolerance for these outdated systems finally ran out.

Not only were workers being forced into low-paying jobs, but the king had also implemented a poll tax to help fund military operations, and that was where people's patience snapped. The tax was high and took a large portion of workers' already limited resources.

Eventually, some citizens in England decided not to pay the tax. The king sent out tax collectors to different villages, but they came back empty-handed. In an attempt to keep his power, he decided to send soldiers out in the hopes of collecting the taxes, but again, he was denied. However, the damage had been done, and the peasants had had enough.

On June 2nd, 1381, a group of over sixty thousand people marched to London. They came from communities all over England and were led by a man named Wat Tyler. As they made their way into the capital, they burned down any government buildings and official documents they could get their hands on. They were particularly interested in destroying tax records.

As the crowd entered the streets of London, the mission became a little diluted. Some seemed eager to simply create mayhem, and violence and mischief broke out. However, there were many who still had their initial purpose in mind, and the king eventually agreed to meet with Wat.

The meeting went well. King Richard probably realized he was out of options and agreed to the demands of the workers. The two men made an agreement that the crowd would go home. Unfortunately, some members of the revolt had other plans.

While Wat Tyler and the king were in their meeting, a group went to the Tower of London, where they viciously murdered the archbishop of Canterbury and the treasurer. Upon learning of this, the king was understandably terrified, but he agreed to meet Wat one more time. This time, the meeting was also attended by the same rebels who had committed the murders at the Tower of London, as well as the mayor of London, Sir William Walworth.

Although the king seemed open to hearing the rebels' demands, the mayor quickly grew violent, and he ended up lashing out and stabbing Wat in the neck.

Wat was taken to hospital, where he was assassinated. However, despite the killing, the king did end up agreeing to the new demands, and the rebels dispersed.

While the revolt itself was over, the peasants did not end up getting what they had hoped for. While the king ended up removing the poll tax, he backtracked on all of his other promises, and workers soon found themselves once again forced into low-paying labor jobs.

While the working class didn't gain all the victories they were hoping for, it wasn't a completely unhappy ending for them. Because it took so long for the population to go back to pre-pandemic levels, many landowners were eventually forced into paying higher wages out of necessity. So, even if some of the rebels in the Peasants' Revolt didn't get to enjoy that, at least some of their descendants might have.

Inflation

Just as the world is currently experiencing a spike in inflation, so did people living during and after subsequent waves of the Black Death. It wasn't just landowners who were dealing with a spike in costs because of the pandemic. Everyone felt the squeeze. Trading, which had become fairly commonplace, suddenly became a dangerous occupation. Traveling increased a person's risk for disease, and not only that, but many cities were incredibly strict about letting traders in and out. They might be ostracized or face weeks of isolation just to get the chance to sell their products.

Because of this, the cost of almost everything went up, which meant lots of people struggled to afford the daily necessities.

Art

When people have no hope left or are trying to discern meaning in the midst of an unimaginably difficult experience, they often turn to art. Because the Black Death kept the world in its grip for so long, there were large periods where artists constantly had the thought of the disease in their minds.

Indeed, both the Renaissance and the Baroque periods of artistic expression happened while the bubonic plague was still ravaging the world. It's a great testament to how necessary and important art is, even in the face of death.

Of course, religion was also a very important part of life during this time, and many artists used their art to try to answer questions they had about God or what the afterlife might look like. Some even used their art in an attempt to convert sinners and bring them into the church. After all, many believed that the plague was a punishment for the sins of people, and it was thought that if enough people were good children of God, then the sickness would disappear.

For many artists, their work during this time was highly dominated by images of death. This is a natural response when one is experiencing grief, and art is often used as a way to process the traumatic events one experiences. However, that doesn't make the pieces themselves any less troubling to see.

One such painting is the *Citizens of Tournai Bury Their Dead* by Pierart dou Tielt, a Belgian artist.

Part of Citizens of Tournai Bury Their Dead.
https://commons.wikimedia.org/wiki/File:Burying_Plague_Victims_of_Tournai.jpg

Some depictions of death were morbid, but others were regarded as humorous, at least at the time. This is true of The Triumph of Death with the Dance of Death. This image features several people, as well as skeletons, dancing around the Queen of Death. The queen stands on top of a coffin that contains the pope and the emperor, a reminder that the plague was capable of killing everyone, even the rich and the powerful.

In the painting, the people dancing offer the queen gifts and all manner of riches, but she doesn't want them. All she wants is their lives. While it may seem strange to us now, a wicked queen who could never be satisfied was seen as entertaining. However, it also demonstrates something else. In the image, the living are dancing with the dead, which offers up the idea that even if you're about to die, you should still love and enjoy life while you can.

Another similarly named but far less amusing painting, *The Triumph of Death* by Pieter Bruegel the Elder, depicts the grim realities of the plague. In it, you see a small village that has been completely destroyed by the disease. Dead bodies litter the ground, and all around the village are scenes of fires and abandoned or quarantined ships. While it might seem extreme, that really was what some communities faced. The Black Death killed extremely fast, and sometimes, the bodies would pile up so quickly that the authorities didn't know how to handle it. That was, of course, if anyone in an authoritative position was still alive.

The Triumph of Death.
https://commons.wikimedia.org/wiki/File:The_Triumph_of_Death_by_Pieter_Bruegel_the_Elder.jpg

Although there are several notable artworks that were created during the plague, we'll leave you thinking about one final piece. It's titled *Human Fragility* and was painted by Salvator Rosa in 1656. In it, Rosa paints an image of his child and his mistress. Death is nearby, cowering over his son. It signifies the loss of his child and the shortness of life. One can only imagine what these artists must have been experiencing when they created these works.

While many of the artworks made during the Black Death were certainly depressing, there were also many celebrating the joy of life and how precious and fleeting it is. These works provide a look into the minds of people who experienced these times and what they must have been thinking.

Tombstones created during the Black Death can also offer insights into the artistic expression of the time. While there were many who chose to have peacefully sleeping figures as the sculptures atop their tombs, there were others who chose much more graphic images. Some chose to have their tombs adorned with an image of Death himself. Morbid, yes, but perhaps fitting given the circumstances.

Antisemitism

As was mentioned earlier, the Black Death gave rise to a wave of antisemitism across Europe. Thousands of Jewish people were killed by mob attacks or by barricading Jewish people into buildings or pits and burning them alive. Although many historians have claimed that Jews were slaughtered because people falsely blamed them for being the origin of the Black Death, there are others who contest this idea.

This is because antisemitism was already rampant throughout Europe, and many Christian communities were already eager to rid their towns or villages of those with different religious beliefs. Persecution against the Jewish people had already been happening for centuries, so it's certainly possible that the only reason the Black Death was ever connected with the influx of hate crimes was because it was a convenient excuse. One of the most persistent lies about how the Jewish people were responsible for the Black Death was because they had supposedly poisoned wells, ensuring that the disease would spread through cities via the drinking water. This, aside from being a blatant falsehood, was also a very weak and illogical explanation for the origins of the plague. First of all, where would they have gotten the plague to poison the wells to begin with, and second, why on earth would they poison the very water they themselves had to drink? But, of course, many people don't need logic to fuel their hatred. Just a tiny wisp of a story will do.

While murders of Jews happened all across Europe, the most concentrated massacres happened in Germany, a bleak foreshadowing of the genocide that would happen there hundreds of years later.

An image of Jews being burned during the Black Death.
https://commons.wikimedia.org/wiki/File:Doutielt1.jpg

Many of these attacks were led by Christian governments and churches. Eager to keep control of their communities, they made up terrible lies that Jewish people were plotting against the Christians and, therefore, needed to be disposed of. It was said that Jews were tortured into giving false confessions to crimes they never committed as another way to "justify" the attacks against them.

A term you might commonly hear mentioned when learning about the antisemitic attacks during the Black Death is "pogrom." A pogrom is a word that is Russian in origin. It refers to a violent mob or riot that is created with the express purpose of killing or banishing a particular religious or ethnic group. Pogroms are overwhelmingly enacted against members of the Jewish community.

Of course, the Jewish community fought back, but they were often overpowered. In a famous act of resistance, the Jews in Mainz, Germany, managed to fight back against the mob that was after them. They even managed to kill two hundred of their attackers. However, they were soon overwhelmed. Realizing they were facing a certain death, they chose to lock themselves in their homes and set themselves on fire rather than die at the hands of their attackers. Over six thousand Jewish people died there, and that was just one of many places where they were attacked.

Over the course of the Black Death, Jewish communities, which had had close to four hundred in numbers all over Europe before the pandemic, were reduced by half.

Again, the major correlation between Jews and the Black Death is simply that the Black Death presented antisemitic Christians with a convenient excuse for them to exercise their hatred. It is very likely that there were many people who had a clear understanding that there was no validity to the claim that the Jews were responsible for the Black Death. But many people would have circulated the lie on purpose with the simple desire of fueling the fire and encouraging more people to lash out against the Jewish community.

There were some who attempted to stop the attacks on the Jewish community. Pope Clement VI attempted to point out the irrationality of Jews starting the plague themselves. However, there were many others who encouraged the massacres and others who even managed to profit from it. The Holy Roman Empire agreed to the massacre of Jewish people as long as they received a payoff from the sale of all the personal belongings that were taken from the murdered families.

Religion

While we'll go further into the impact religion had during the Black Death in the next chapter, it's worth mentioning here that religious communities actually lost a little bit of power during this time.

Some people accepted that death was right around the corner and turned to a life of debauchery and excess. They stopped worrying about the societal expectations of the time and instead chose to spend their remaining days enjoying drink and merriment.

There were others who lost their faith in God. As more and more people fell prey to the hands of death, many people questioned their faith and how they could possibly love a God who cared so little for them. Even if the plague was a punishment for their sins, there were some who felt the punishment had gone too far and looked for solace in other forms of spirituality.

This turned a lot of people onto the idea of mysticism and old folk stories as a way of trying to make sense of what was happening around them. While religion still held strong across the world, there was a definite pulling away and a search for deeper meaning during this time.

With such a tremendous loss of and disruption to life, Europe was sent into an unstable condition that lasted for generations. It was a long time before the population stabilized, and it is very likely that anyone who survived the bubonic plague was forever changed. With so many deaths, it is very unlikely that there wasn't anyone alive who didn't have several people who they were close to die. People lost their friends, family, government officials, and religious leaders. Some villages were almost completely wiped out. The full extent of the Black Death's impact cannot possibly be comprehended by those who didn't live through it.

Chapter 5: The Role of Religion in the Age of the Black Death

There were three main religious groups in Europe during the Black Death: Catholics, Muslims, and Jews. Each religion was heavily impacted by the plague and dealt with it in different ways. Let's look first at Catholicism. Now, of course, Catholicism is a branch of Christianity, so we may, at times, use the terms interchangeably. But it is important to note that while all Catholic people are Christian, that doesn't mean the opposite is true. However, the most dominant form of Christianity at the time in Europe was Catholicism, so that is the term that is often used in this book.

Even before the start of the Black Death, the Catholic Church was facing some difficulties. While many might strongly associate the church as having its headquarters in Rome, during the early 1300s, a massive change took place that certainly ruffled feathers in several communities.

The church had been stationed in Rome for quite some time, but in 1309, the political situation there had become volatile. There had already been fractures within the institution itself, but one thing seemed to be clear: staying in Rome wasn't a viable option. Instead, it was decided that the pope at the time, Pope Clement V, would relocate to Avignon, France. This created quite an uproar among Catholic communities, particularly in England and Germany. It was thought that the move to France had damaged the integrity of the church and created a situation where the pope was more invested in the desires of the

French monarchy rather than the needs of the faith itself.

The Avignon papacy lasted for quite some time, with seven popes in total residing there, and the trouble it caused cannot be overstated. In fact, it was the move to Avignon that eventually led to the Great Schism (also known as the Papal Schism or Western Schism), which was when three different popes operated at the same time, causing great division for several decades.

The Black Death arrived several years before the schism took place, but it is worth mentioning so you can better understand the kind of tension that was simmering in Europe at the time.

The popes in Avignon were attempting to modernize the church, but the Black Death put a damper on many of their plans. The death tolls were so high, particularly in Rome, that many began to feel resentful toward the church for its decisions.

Catholics were firm in their belief that not only was the Black Death contagious, but it was also a punishment for one's sins. However, Muslims had a different response.

Looking at examples of what was happening in the Middle East, Professor Michael W. Dols wrote that the general feeling was that the Black Death was not a result of one's sins and that the response to it was one of prayer and humility.

Large processions and ceremonies took place, and members of the faith were encouraged to be extra pious. Interestingly, it seemed that Muslims did not support the idea that the plague itself was contagious. They held the belief that the sickness was a gift and would transport the sick to paradise after their death. Because it was thought that each sick person had been chosen by God individually, it was deemed unnecessary to isolate or quarantine a victim. Instead, Muslims were encouraged to remain with the sick.

Sadly, there is little research available on how the Jewish population felt about the Black Death or how they responded to it. Because they were facing such extreme violence, mainly at the hands of Catholics, most of the research that exists is focused on their persecution, not their response to the disease.

For a long time, there was a persistent rumor that Jewish communities suffered fewer deaths from the plague than other communities; however, fact-checking this theory has proved difficult. It has been suggested that this was due to the strict diet and cleanliness standards that Jews were expected to adhere to in their faith, but historians have rightly pointed out that even the most rigorous sanitization standards wouldn't stop fleas or animals from spreading the disease. Instead, it is much more likely that a rumor was started that Jewish people were not as affected by the disease as a way to continue to fuel the idea that they were somehow responsible for the Black Death in the first place.

Now that we've covered the major religions that were active during the Black Death, let's dive deeper into how each group responded to it.

Rise of the Flagellant Movement

While we briefly touched on the flagellant movement earlier in this book, what we didn't cover is that the response wasn't always so extreme.

In fact, Catholics' initial responses to the plague weren't all that different from the Muslims. While their beliefs about why the Black Death had descended upon them were different, both groups doubled down on their commitment to God. Catholics took to the streets and led processions throughout cities and villages. They built shrines to God and the Virgin Mary and prayed continuously.

There were many who believed that certain amulets or charms were capable of keeping them safe, so it wasn't uncommon to see Catholics carrying these items with them.

These processions continued for quite some time, even after it was understood that the disease was contagious and that spending too much time together in groups was dangerous.

However, after several months of peaceful processions, the faithful began to lose faith in their churches. They couldn't understand why God hadn't yet freed them from the clutches of such an insidious disease and became convinced that the church wasn't doing enough. Something more drastic needed to be done. This was when the flagellant movement began to gain traction.

The movement seemed to originate in Austria in 1348 but soon spread to other parts of Europe. Despite the chaotic nature of the group, its members were remarkably organized.

Someone would be appointed leader or "master" of the group, and they would march the other flagellants into different towns, often ending their march at a church. This group would often be several hundred people strong. During the march, they would often wear long cloaks and crosses, but upon arriving at their destination, they would strip off their clothes until they had nothing covering their upper half.

A 15th- or 16th-century woodcut of flagellants.
https://commons.wikimedia.org/wiki/File:Nuremberg_chronicles_-_Flagellants_(CCXVr).jpg

At this point, they would begin chanting and saying fervent prayers while taking out whips that were typically knotted with pieces of metal. They would beat themselves with the whips until they were bloody and eventually fell to their knees. Some groups would then form themselves into the image of a cross on the ground while the master read out a letter calling on other members of the community to repent. It was also common practice for the flagellants to take positions that signified some of the accepted sins, such as murder or adultery.

This whole process would then be repeated in the next town. While you may not think this would be appealing to many, the flagellants managed to build quite a following. The flagellants were angry at what they felt were inadequacies of the church, and this was their form of rebellion. Many people also viewed joining the flagellants as a way to avoid the plague. They felt the church wasn't doing enough, and this was seen as a valid form of prevention or cure. There was also something appealing about the organization. The group was very ritualistic, and in a world that had become increasingly chaotic, something was reassuring about having a routine. It didn't seem to matter that the routine involved brutally beating oneself.

Unfortunately, this group didn't just punish themselves. While they believed that the Black Death was a punishment for their sins, that didn't seem to stop them from blaming other groups for it. The flagellants were instrumental in persecuting the Jewish people and several other groups. They had quite an appetite for blood, and that was very appealing to people who had lots of anger and nowhere else to put it.

At first, the church put up little resistance to the flagellants. While their methods were extreme, they seemed to be giving people purpose and order, and it didn't initially seem like the movement was presenting a challenge to Catholic values.

However, as time went on, the church became increasingly concerned about the popularity of the flagellant movement. It was seen as operating in direct contradiction to what the church stood for, and citizens of various towns and cities often acted in ways that were not approved by the church. People fed and watered the flagellants and invited them into their homes. Sometimes, the bells of local churches were even rung in celebration of the flagellants' arrival, an act that was done against the church's express wishes.

The flagellant movement was unique in that it was accessible to people of all classes. While only the wealthy were able to afford certain treatments, such as leeches or emeralds, anyone who was tired of the Catholic faith could join the flagellants at no cost. The flagellants were people's chance at salvation. And if nothing else, they were seen as excellent entertainment. Just as ancient Rome enjoyed watching gladiators engage in combat, villagers looked forward to the exciting displays of public song, dance, and violence during the Middle Ages.

While the flagellants eventually descended into chaos, at the beginning, they had a set of strict rules that they were all expected to adhere to.

1. No bathing.
2. No interaction with someone of the opposite sex.
3. No changing of their clothes, no matter how bloody or sweaty they ended up.
4. They had to have whipped themselves for eight hours over a certain period of time.

5. They had to pay a certain amount of money toward nourishment each day.

Some groups also planned their processions to match up with the age of Jesus Christ when he was crucified.

Pope Clement VI explicitly condemned the movement. He attempted to stop their attacks on minorities, but support for persecution of the Jewish community and other groups was too strong for his objections to have any impact. However, the church's opposition and eventual expulsion of many of its members was the beginning of the end for the movement. Within a year of the pope publicly denouncing them, their numbers began to fade.

The Black Death wasn't the first time flagellation had gained popularity, and it wasn't the last. But the movement during the plague was likely the biggest of its kind that will ever be seen in history.

Another reason the flagellant movement might have gained the popularity that it did was the lack of access to holy figures. Many priests died or were forced to close the doors to their churches. And traveling to places of worship became difficult in the face of so much chaos. Because of this, worshipers were no longer able to confess their sins to a listening ear and be absolved.

Confession of one's sins is a major element of the Catholic faith, and the loss of this routine was devastating. People started to confess to doctors or friends, people who could not absolve them. And from this issue sprang a thirst for something called indulgences, which brings us to a surprising element of the impact of religion during the Black Death: profit.

It should not be news to hear that some people are happy to profit off of other people's desperation and misery. In fact, tragedy can be an excellent time for people with no morals to make some money.

Indulgences were special documents that forgave people for their sins. They were handed out by the pope and were typically reserved for people who had served the church in some way, such as participating in a crusade. However, due to the unusual circumstances of the Black Death, indulgences became a way for people to receive the relief they had formally only been able to attain at confession.

Anyone with enough funds started purchasing indulgences from traveling sellers. Some indulgences were real, and some were not. Either way, it was a profitable business.

There was also an influx in the selling of religious symbols, such as amulets, which claimed to help protect the wearer from the plague. Whether or not the person selling these so-called protective items was actually part of the church isn't particularly relevant, as they were still taking advantage of poor souls who were doing anything they could to protect themselves.

Even in death, Catholics were willing to pay for the hope of a better afterlife. At the time, it was thought that a Mass held in their name would absolve their sins even if they hadn't been able to achieve that goal while they were still alive. Because of this, it became fashionable to pay to hold Mass after someone's death. This was very lucrative for bad actors willing to take advantage of people and very trying for members of the church who had the best intentions but were then required to perform multiple ceremonies each day.

The search for profit during this period was also present within Muslim communities as well. So many people were dying that gravedigging became a very lucrative profession, so many specifically sought out that line of work. However, not everyone was seeking compensation from the dead. There were also many volunteers at these mass gravesites who seemed to view the work as their responsibility to the dead.

It became common for mosques to hold mass funerals. The death tolls were so high that it was almost impossible to hold funerals for just one individual at a time.

Just as was true of Catholics, some Muslims also turned to mysticism in the hopes of answering some of the impossible questions they had surrounding the plague that had taken over their lives. There were some who believed that the Black Death was not the work of Allah but was instead the result of the evil deity known as Ahriman, or servants of the deity. Because of this, there was also a surge of demand for amulets and special charms that they hoped would protect themselves against this evil.

Religion has played an important role in major crises throughout time. However, the bubonic plague was a true test of many people's faith. For some, it was a comfort, one of the only places where people could feel like they truly had someone looking out for them. For others, it became something that they questioned and eventually lost faith in.

The rise of the flagellants and the brutal persecution of Jewish communities highlighted the darkness that is also present in the most dominant religions in the world. While there were many who sought peace and kindness during such a difficult time, there were many others who purposefully pursued violence and destruction, often hiding behind religion in order to execute their desires.

While many questioned their faith during this time, the desire to be seen favorably by one's God and have a good afterlife seemed to be too tempting for the masses to ignore. While religious institutions certainly had their fair share of difficulties during this time, they also enjoyed enormous profits and support. As is still true today, there are many people who look to their faith for answers when faced with unimaginable catastrophes.

Chapter 6: The Plague Disappears

While it's true that the bubonic plague is still active today, its power eventually dissipated to the point where it was generally accepted to have "disappeared."

Quarantine

One of the most powerful tools used to combat the spread of the plague was the use of quarantining, which we've already covered in quite some detail. But what might be an important detail to include is that it took quite a long time for quarantine measures to be put in place all around the world.

For example, one of the first documented cases of a ship quarantine happened in 1377 in the city now known as Dubrovnik. The Black Death was already spreading rapidly, and the quarantine there was put in place regardless of whether or not anyone on board was exhibiting symptoms.

However, quarantines didn't become common everywhere until a few hundred years later during subsequent plague outbreaks. In England, quarantines of personal residences weren't implemented until the early 1500s. People were required to hang bales of hay outside their homes to let their community know they were sick. Anyone who had contact with someone infected with the Black Death had to carry a white pole with them whenever they left their house to let others know there was a chance they were carrying the sickness.

Eventually, it became standard practice to shut people into their homes when they were sick. While some places simply expected people to follow the rules, there were other cities that took much more aggressive approaches. When the plague took down a large portion of the population of London during the 1600s, people were either barricaded into their homes or forced into places called pesthouses. It didn't matter if there were healthy people still inside the home; if one person was sick, then everyone would be treated as though they were sick. This was necessary because of the highly contagious nature of the disease. And, of course, at the time, there were no tests available that could detect the presence of the Black Death before symptoms appeared. Their homes would be kept guarded, and anyone who attempted to escape could possibly face death.

Of course, this was not a perfect system. Many people managed to get out of quarantined homes without detection. Plus, although armed guards were used, there weren't enough of them to guard every residence where a sick person lived. So, as a result, sickness was still able to pass through communities quite rapidly.

However, quarantining was definitely a powerful tool in limiting the spread of the plague. In fact, it was so effective that it is still in use today. Just a few years ago, a cruise ship carrying passengers who were sick was kept quarantined for weeks to prevent the spread of disease. Many people have also quarantined when they are sick themselves, which means they are not able to pass illnesses on to as many people as they might if they had gone about their regular lives.

Quarantining isn't just a measure that is useful in the prevention of deadly plagues; it can also be used to help prevent the spread of the common cold. Of course, this type of quarantining doesn't require a hay bale or a cross to be present outside your door, but staying home from work when sick not only can help heal you faster but also help protect your friends and colleagues from catching a cold as well.

Sanitization

The truth is there is no clear answer for why the Black Death eventually died down to a level where it was no longer a major threat. However, there are several theories as to why it began to diminish after hundreds of years of havoc. One of the most likely reasons is the implementation of sanitization systems around the world. Let's take a look at what changes were made and how that impacted not just the spread of the Black Death but also life in general.

As you'll recall, for many years, it was thought that the Black Death had been delivered by God. It was also thought that bad-smelling air was the culprit. Because of this, a lot of the general health and safety measures we now know were not even on anyone's mind in the Middle Ages. It wasn't until the 1700s that disease began to be linked to unsanitary conditions.

Without cities, it might have taken longer for the world to realize that exposure to waste was hazardous to one's health. In small towns, there were fewer people, so even though their attitude toward waste was similar to that of big cities, it didn't pile up in the same way. But by the mid-1800s, the lack of proper sanitization was starting to become a really big issue.

Now, it's important to note that different countries had different approaches to waste. Ancient Rome and Egypt are both examples of places that had developed versions of sewage systems, and some of this knowledge was kept through the years and expanded into other countries. However, even with some systems in place, there was no system that processed or cleansed wastewater. Sewage would generally just be tossed into whatever water source was nearby.

This was a major issue in many countries around the world. Wastewater containing sewage and other toxins would either be dumped into rivers and oceans or sometimes just thrown on the street. Garbage also had no proper method of collection and would typically just be abandoned or sometimes burned.

It wasn't really until the smell of cities and the death toll from a multitude of diseases got really bad that steps were taken to bring in adequate sanitization systems. Of course, there were some people who had championed change for a long time or were instrumental in creating some of these systems. Let's take a look at one of these figures.

Sir John Pringle

Sir John Pringle was an English physician who studied disease. He studied in England and the Netherlands, and his particular area of interest was the spread of disease within hospitals and army camps.

In 1752, he published *Observations on the Diseases of the Army*, which helped lay the groundwork for systems that are still utilized in the military today. A major note of his was the importance of sanitization in military camps, particularly the use of proper restroom facilities and how crucial it was to keep camps as dry as possible. Drainage systems were put in place, and it was highly encouraged that the military stay away from marshes whenever possible.

Sir Pringle also encouraged the use of adequate ventilation systems in hospitals. As you may recall, the demand for proper ventilation has dominated news stories for the past few years. While there have been many suggestions and theories put forward about public health throughout the thousands of years that humans have been on this earth, it's incredible to think that some of the conclusions that were drawn in the past still stand the test of time. Ventilation and staying away from wastewater continue to be two of the best techniques that can help keep a population safe today.

Pringle's work also set the stage for what is known as health surveillance data. This tracks not only diseases related to sanitization and geographic location but also looks at childhood diseases to determine which individuals or groups might be most at risk. This type of data has been instrumental in helping to reduce diseases within the military.

You have to understand that not only was the Black Death still an issue, but there were several other diseases that were commonplace until sanitization took priority. These included typhoid fever, tuberculosis, cholera, and smallpox. In fact, at one point, things got so bad that half of all children within the working class in England died before the age of five. While people in the 1300s perhaps didn't have enough resources to study the spread of disease, a couple of hundred years later, there was a much better understanding of disease. For example, the primary ideas of germ theory had been put forth by Girolamo Fracastoro in 1546, but it wasn't until the 1800s that the idea really took off with a greater understanding of bacteria and how they could cause enormous damage even when they weren't visible to the naked eye. So, an advancement in scientific understanding was a major reason why there were such strides made in sanitization, but there was another reason as well: cities smelled bad. Really bad.

Waste and sewage littered the streets and waterways, and lower-class neighborhoods were overcrowded and filthy. The death and sickness rates were so high that populations were being affected, and many people had to drop out of the workplace. This was particularly evident during the Industrial Revolution when the population in cities grew due to the proliferation of warehouses. With so much production happening, many businesses required large workforces, and thousands of people rushed into big cities in search of jobs. While this improved the lives of many, it also forced large portions of the population into slums and greatly increased the amount of waste.

With the advancements made in science and medicine and an increasingly urgent need for better systems to prevent diseases, a public health proposal came along known as the Sanitary Idea.

For some time, people had been examining the impact of poor sanitation on public health, and it was Villerme, a physician in Paris, who noted that the lower classes seemed to suffer disease at much higher rates than the upper classes. This had been discovered after many unsuccessful attempts to find out why certain areas had such high rates of disease. When things like climate and elevation turned up nothing, he connected economic factors with rates of disease and realized there was an extremely strong correlation.

Around the same time, Sir Edwin Chadwick, who worked as a social reformer, also began looking into these issues. He eventually published a report called "Report into the Sanitary Conditions of the Labouring Populations of Great Britain."

Now, sadly, a lot of these advancements were not necessarily made out of caring for the health of the general population. Instead, Chadwick pointed out that such rampant disease greatly reduced the availability of workers. It was also observed that a sick person cost the government more than a healthy one. So, one could certainly argue that the sanitary measures that were eventually put in place were done in an attempt to protect capitalism and not because the government cared about the health of the working class.

Regardless, these reports did signal a change in public sanitization. Paris and London were the earliest adopters of these improved systems, but cities around the world began to implement better sanitation systems over the next hundred years.

This point in history brought new awareness to the important role that engineers could play in public health. While much of the work surrounding the treatment and prevention of disease was left to scientists, it was engineers who had to design and implement these intricate systems.

A fascinating element to all of this is that the actual science behind a lot of this thinking still wasn't correct. The concept of miasma, which we covered in Chapter 3, was still in vogue during this time. Chadwick himself was a believer in this theory. But of course, many unsanitary conditions did smell, so while the smell wasn't the cause of disease, many of the strategies that got rid of the smell also got rid of a lot of the bacteria that caused these illnesses.

The Sanitary Idea was enormously successful and drastically reduced rates of infection. Along with the introduction of modern sanitary systems, a slew of legislation was passed as well. This legislation put certain rules in place in terms of sewage and waste disposal. It also put requirements on landlords to provide certain standards of living for their tenants.

The success of these ideas has been demonstrated throughout history. People living in clean spaces with good ventilation and proper nutrition are generally healthier. People living in cramped, impoverished areas or living through periods of war often fall victim to disease.

Chadwick's ideas were not immediately accepted. However, the severity of the situation at the time was enough to convince the government to implement them. In his report, for example, it was shown that the average age of death for laborers was sixteen years old. Tradesmen fared just a little better. Their average age of death was twenty-two. Having no other solutions available to them, governments around the world started to improve sanitation and living quarters. The almost immediate success of these changes created a ripple effect, and soon, "being clean" was seen as a sign of virtue and success.

While the shift toward more sanitary living conditions was certainly a smart one, this time period created an unusual issue that still persists in society today. This is the idea that cleanliness indicates moral superiority. In some cases, people believe that cleanliness can even bring one closer to God. However, the idea of cleanliness doesn't always indicate whether or not something is sanitary. People living in poverty may not always have the resources available to properly wash themselves or their clothing. They may also not be able to clean or repair their homes and businesses as well as someone in a higher tax bracket.

However, this difference in appearance does not mean that the individual with less money is unable to maintain proper waste disposal, which is really what the biggest issue is in terms of preventing disease.

Nevertheless, there has been unfair discrimination placed upon people who are unable to keep up with the standards of cleanliness that have become a signal of morality. This is a rather fascinating shift in thinking from hundreds of years earlier when people were more than comfortable spreading feces or putting bare chicken bottoms all over their bodies!

Advancement of Germ Theory

As the 1800s wore on, there were many scientific advancements made that helped shape the course of disease treatment and understanding. One of the most pivotal discoveries made during this time was by Louis Pasteur, a French chemist and biologist. Pasteur was studying food and drink and examined possible reasons for why they spoiled even though nothing visible had happened to them.

After some period of study, he concluded that this must be caused by microorganisms, bacteria that were too small for the human eye to see without the help of a powerful microscope. As you may have already guessed, it was because of him that pasteurization is a common practice today. Pasteurization has saved countless lives and has extended the life of food for people all over the world.

Pasteur helped set the stage for an understanding of where the Black Death came from. Without this knowledge, a treatment could never have been developed, and we might still be dealing with ongoing waves of the disease.

Of course, the waves of the pandemic were much less severe in the 1800s than when they first hit European shores back in 1337, but that doesn't mean the Black Death had disappeared. It was still responsible for claiming countless lives, and any advancements brought the world one step closer to ending it once and for all.

Immunity

There's one final element to the disappearance of the Black Death that's worth mentioning before we close out this chapter. That is the topic of immune systems and their role in diminishing the impact of the plague.

This is an area that has been studied, but given that the worst waves of the Black Death happened so long ago and there have been so many changes since then, it is hard to draw any definite conclusions. However, the topic of immunity is still worth mentioning when talking about the Black Death and disease in general.

With the exception of a few different disorders, the human body is typically made up of twenty-three pairs of chromosomes (making forty-six in total). Within these chromosomes lies our genes, which are made up of DNA. Our genes are basically little instruction manuals for our bodies. They determine our features, such as the color of our eyes and the size of our nose. But they also determine how our body responds to disease and environmental factors.

The Black Death is incredibly aggressive. Before treatments became available, there was a very high chance that anyone who contracted it would be dead within three days. But there were some who survived it. And there were others who never got it at all, even though they were exposed to it multiple times. Why is that?

One thought is that people who avoided or survived the Black Death might have had specific gene variants that protected against the disease. A variant may also be referred to as a mutation that can occur in a gene. These mutations can then be passed down through the family line, which means that future generations may be born with natural immunity against something like the Black Death.

This is a phenomenon that is known as natural selection. It has been extensively studied in animal populations. While many people like to prescribe the idea of "survival of the fittest" to situations like this, it actually has nothing to do with fitness. This has been demonstrated many times when the world has faced other pandemics. People who had no prior history of disease, exercised frequently, and had a healthy diet were often just as susceptible to the disease as people who did not follow such strict diet and fitness regimens. Of course, the situation is very different for people who already have a disability or compromised immune system.

Natural selection is something that happens because people happen to be born with certain genes. Also, just because one person might have a gene variant that naturally protects them against the bubonic plague does not mean that that same variant can protect them from any other diseases. It just depends on whether certain mutations are helpful at protecting against the specific bacterium present in whichever disease is prevalent at the time.

Recently, two scientists, Dr. Hendrik Poinar from McMaster University in Canada and Dr. Luis Barreiro from the University of Chicago in the United States, set out to research this exact topic. They managed to access the remains of five hundred people who lived before, during, and after the first wave of the Black Death in Europe back in the

1300s. They procured most of the samples from cemeteries in England and a few from locations in Denmark. Their final conclusions were drawn from the samples of two hundred people.

The way this research was conducted was by looking at specific variants that appeared to have either increased or decreased dramatically after the Black Death swept through the area. Dr. Poinar and Dr. Barreiro ended up observing four variants of interest. After further investigation, they found that there was one particular variant located near the gene ERAP2, which is responsible for the production of a protein that helps a pathogen protein break into smaller pieces. This then supports the immune system in being more efficient at noticing infections. People who had two of this specific variant had an even better chance of fighting off infection. This was because the macrophages (a type of white blood cell that can kill microorganisms and help support healthy immune systems) were better at attacking the bacterium that caused the Black Death (*Y. pestis*) with the support of the variant.

Although the variant in question seemed to help protect against the Black Death, it had its downside as well, as it created an elevated risk of Crohn's disease. There was also another variant that seemed to offer enhanced protection against the Black Death, but that variant also came with a great risk of two types of autoimmune diseases. So, while the populations affected by the Black Death might have developed better resistance to it over the generations, natural selection might mean that much of the world also became more likely to end up with certain autoimmune diseases.

Many questions remain about why and how the Black Death disappeared, but that is often the case with horrific and mystifying pandemics that come in and out of our lives. What we do know is that the plague reshaped the course of history and resulted in some long-lasting social changes for the better.

Chapter 7: Shaping the Course of European History

There's no way to know what the world would have looked like had the Black Death never happened. Instead, all we can do is observe all the changes that happened as a result of it.

One of the biggest changes that resulted from the bubonic plague was a change in class systems. While we've already talked in some detail about the plague-affected labor, there are a few terms that we haven't yet covered. Labor is one of the most studied areas of this time period, and what happened as a result of labor shortages set the stage for labor disputes that still happen in a similar way today. Let's get into a few terms you should know about.

Feudal System

The feudal system, or feudalism, was in place in Europe for centuries. It began sometime in the 700s and remained a powerful system up into the 1400s. Although this system began to diminish around that time, it continued to remain in place in some areas for another four hundred years!

This system was put in place to provide the upper class with a way to exert and retain their power. Under the feudal system, parcels of land, known as fiefs, would be loaned out to a tenant. However, instead of just paying rent (which was definitely a requirement as well), it was expected that whoever was occupying the land would do the landowner's bidding. This could mean a wide range of services. A large reason for developing the feudal system was to ensure a strong enough army would be at the ready. Someone occupying a fief was required to join in any military operations that were required of them.

This system created a huge imbalance in society. Instead of laws being put in place by an elected government, almost all the power was put in the hands of the individual lords in charge of the fiefs. They held the ultimate power over the people below them.

Now, you may be wondering why some people within the feudal system simply couldn't come and go as they pleased. Unfortunately, it wasn't quite as simple as that. There definitely were some people who were in a comfortable enough position to decide whether or not they wanted to pay a higher rent or exchange services for the land they lived on. This exchange sometimes even happens today. Someone might be a building manager in exchange for free rent or offer to do repairs or some gardening in exchange for a rent reduction. However, at the bottom of the change were serfs.

Serfdom was the lowest level of the feudal system. This was when people were born onto these specific plots of land or were paid such extraordinarily low wages that they had no hope of ever advancing in the world. Because of this, they were forever tied to the lords who owned the land and were forced into doing whatever work was demanded of them, even if it was completely unreasonable.

This was the system that was in place when the Black Death first sailed into port. Serfs were not technically bound to a person, but they were bound to the land. They cultivated their own food and necessities but were obligated to give most of their harvest to their lord. The lords also determined how they managed the land and where they milled their wheat.

Not only was the work a serf did determined by their lord, but so was everything else. Serfs were not allowed to leave their area of residence or change their occupation unless they received permission from their lord. Not only that, but they couldn't even marry someone of their own choosing unless their lord approved of it. Generally, a serf's only hope at freedom was through escape. Lords were notoriously brutal and not generally known to be compassionate.

Once the worker population shrank, the feudal system began to crash, and the lower classes finally began to make the earnings they deserved. Of course, we have covered the rest of that in an earlier chapter, but now you know more about the exact conditions landowners were attempting to force people back into.

The end of the feudal system was one of the biggest changes that resulted from the Black Death. The exploitation of workers is sadly one that continues to this day, but the peasant revolt helped to undo some of the power landowners once had. Today, most of the places where feudalism was once the norm now have strict rules against serfdom and give much more power to workers. France, in particular, is known to have quite a robust working culture. This might not have been the case today if the Black Death had never happened.

Women

Even though the Black Death started hundreds of years ago, it still generates an incredible amount of interest among historians. However, documentation from the time has sometimes been difficult to acquire, and there have been many disagreements on a variety of topics. One such topic is how the Black Death affected the lives of women.

For a long time, the idea was put forth that the years following the first wave of the Black Death were known as the "golden years" for women. This was because so many women, who had very few rights before the pandemic, were suddenly in a position to support themselves and build up their assets. With so many workers dead, landowners would inevitably be willing to turn to anyone to get work done, even if that meant employing women.

However, while it is certainly true that there must have been more job openings available after the first wave, it doesn't follow that landowners would go to women. And if they did, it seems likely that women were handed the short end of the stick.

At the time, it was common for a lot of work to be delivered under short-term contracts. This might mean a weekly contract or even something as short as a day. These contracts were generally more lucrative than the annual contracts that tied a worker to one position and often involved housing. While many men pursued short-term work for higher pay, it seemed that women tended to end up in fixed contracts that gave them less money and less freedom.

The exact reasons for this difference between male and female workers are unclear, but it could be due to the established societal preference for male workers and the uncertainty of whether or not short-term work would be consistently available. Annual work might have paid less, but at least it could provide security to a woman whose position was already precarious.

Of course, it is likely that some women ended up in a better position than others after the arrival of the Black Death, but there doesn't seem to be much evidence to suggest that this happened in large enough numbers to have made a great difference for women in the long term. This is supported by the fact that the rights of women remained fairly unchanged for many years, even after the impact of the Black Death began to lessen. But we still don't know everything about what happened during that time. So, it's nice to imagine that some women saw a benefit after so much darkness.

However, there is one area of a woman's life that did see a positive change due to the pandemic, and that was the issue of inheritance.

Before the Black Death, it was very unusual for women to be able to own land. Most inheritance laws dictated that land and other assets could only be left to a son. If no son had been produced, then the inheritance would be passed on to the next closest male relative.

However, because so many people died during the Black Death, it became impossible to operate under the same inheritance system. Because of this, many women ended up owning land for the first time. Not only that, but some of them were able to own and run their own businesses and even have some decision-making power over who they decided to marry.

However, these new freedoms did not last forever. After the initial panic of the plague had passed, many governments and religious institutions began to claw back the rights they had temporarily granted to women. The idea that men were the only ones capable of running homes or government was still prevalent, and it would be hundreds of years before most women would be able to own property again. For instance, it wasn't until 1900 that laws were passed in every US state that allowed women the right to their own money or the ability to have property in their own name. However, any movement, even if not immediately successful, lays the groundwork for future ones. The freedom that women enjoyed, even if temporary, surely influenced women's rights in the future.

Art

As previously mentioned, artistic expression was incredibly important during the Black Death. During this time, there was a noted increase in motifs of death. A lot of the artwork made during the plague was very dark and, interestingly, much less grand than a lot of the work that had been produced prior to the pandemic.

Architecture

Another area that experienced a drastic change was the design of architecture. As the world gradually began to better understand how the disease moved through the world, there was a need to redesign cities and buildings.

Many cities expanded. A lot of them had grown overcrowded, with many people in the lower classes forced into extremely cramped and unsanitary housing. When the world started to understand that ventilation and good sanitation were important tools to help combat the plague, more housing began to be built to spread out the population. There was also an emphasis on providing larger outdoor spaces within cities, where people could breathe in fresh air without being crammed together inside.

The Black Death also required the construction of several plague hospitals. These were meant to be sanitary, organized buildings where people could be isolated from the healthy and die a dignified death. While not every hospital lived up to these ideals, the outline of these hospitals helped to serve as a blueprint for future medical facilities.

But it wasn't just the design of a city that changed during and after the pandemic. It was the actual buildings themselves.

Before the Black Death began to ravage Europe, architecture had been quite elaborate. French Gothic was the dominant style. It is known for its large pointed arches and windows. Notre-Dame Cathedral is a well-known example of a beautiful French Gothic building. However, after the Black Death, there was a marked decline in this opulent style. Instead, construction trended toward what is now known as Perpendicular Gothic. This style was very different from the style that had been so beloved before. It was quite simple and featured much harsher angles and lines. There were very few decorative embellishments, and buildings took on a rather cold and authoritarian-looking appearance.

Architecture has changed throughout time, and it's not uncommon for trends to shift after a major event, but what's interesting is trying to determine why specific styles came into vogue. There are a few theories.

Some historians suggest that the change in architecture had little to do with the plague at all. It's suggested that perpendicular designs were already becoming fashionable even before the Black Death arrived and that this change was falsely attributed to being a result of the plague instead of a natural change in trends.

Another theory is that this change in architecture was connected to the massive loss of life experienced during the pandemic. It is thought that the shift was due to the loss of experts in the architectural field. French Gothic designs are so elaborate and detailed that it took workers many years to perfect their craft. It is possible that many people with the know-how in these areas died and that to continually build in this style after the Black Death simply wasn't possible.

A third suggested theory regards cost. The plague saw a drastic increase in inflation, as well as a desperate demand for critical workers in areas like agriculture. This might have meant that the construction of beautiful and elaborate buildings was no longer economically feasible. The sharp and angular buildings of the Perpendicular Gothic period could have been the result of cost-cutting labor.

Whatever the reason, Perpendicular Gothic, also eventually known as Tudor architecture, remained the dominant style until the shift to Renaissance architecture in the mid-1500s.

Shift in Beliefs

As was mentioned in Chapter 5, religion played a major role in the response to the Black Death. However, it is unlikely that religious leaders foresaw the dip in faith that resulted from the dreadful disease.

The powerlessness of the church to prevent the Black Death from spreading created a lot of anger and resentment toward God and religious leaders. This divide took quite some time for the church to repair. Its efforts were also hampered because so many priests had died. While it would be inaccurate to say that the church lost its power, it definitely saw a decline in numbers, as many people turned toward other forms of spirituality or to more extremist groups, such as the flagellant movement.

What might be a more accurate statement is that many people lost their belief in the church. The core beliefs of Catholicism remained instilled in the general population of Europe, but a lot of the dissatisfaction was directed at the church. People were looking for solace and the ability to be absolved of their sins, but the steep decline of available clergymen made doing this difficult. While this wasn't within the church's control, it didn't stop Catholics from being angry about it and seeking comfort in whatever ways they could.

To further illustrate the difficulties the Catholic Church found itself in, it's important to talk about how many clergymen died. Across certain parts of England, the number of dead hovered at around 50 percent, while in one diocese in Barcelona, clergymen faced a 60 percent death rate at the peak of the plague. It has even been suggested that leaders of the church were infected and died at higher numbers than the general public due to the fact that they were constantly comforting and praying for the sick.

While the church gradually began to return to its former glory, the shifting ideas about how it should operate had already gone into motion. New congregations were formed, and many Catholics began to redefine their expectations of the church and religion. While not the sole cause, this shift in attitude helped lead to the Reformation in the 1500s. This was a religious revolution that led to the formation of Protestantism, another major branch of Christianity. One of the core beliefs during the beginning of Protestantism was that the Catholic Church was corrupt and had drifted away from the most important values of the faith. Thus, Protestantism was created with the idea of righting the wrongs that had been done and creating a purer faith.

This, of course, led to other independent faith movements. Again, these movements were not in opposition to the idea of God himself but rather the dominant power that had been placed in the hands of the Catholic Church for so long.

The Black Death created enormous shifts in the political, social, and economic landscape of Europe. While many norms shifted during this time, the ones covered in this chapter were some of the most striking and well documented.

Chapter 8: Scientific Advancements in the Wake of the Black Death

The Black Death continues to fascinate scientists and the general public to this very day. For a long time, the cause of it was completely misunderstood. It was seen as a punishment from God or as an evil that had simply floated in on a wave of bad air.

You might also recall the theory of the four humors, which persisted for generations.

However, as time wore on and the bubonic plague continued to come back every few years, there were some who grew understandably skeptical. If the plague really was a punishment from God or was simply the imbalance of fluids within the body, then why didn't it go away after repenting one's sins or draining one's blood?

It took a long time for germ theory to gain significant traction. Throughout the 1600s and 1700s, there had been discussions on the topic. In 1665, Robert Hooke was able to accurately tell the world about how the fruiting structures of molds worked. And just over a decade later, Antoni van Leeuwenhoek discovered bacteria. However, despite these promising discoveries, it would still take over two hundred years for the official cause of the Black Death to be found.

The 19th century is when several major advancements in the understanding of infectious diseases were made. Up until this point, the prevailing theory around disease was that it was the result of something called spontaneous generation.

Spontaneous generation is the idea that life (and bacteria is included within that) could just appear spontaneously. For example, someone who believed in this theory might think that mice would just appear in food that had been left out or that maggots would simply arise out of the flesh of a decaying corpse. This idea that life could arrive spontaneously, sometimes out of non-living matter, was essential in discovering the real cause of how the Black Death worked.

Louis Pasteur wasn't convinced that spontaneous generation was true, so he set out to conduct some experiments to contradict the theory. In one experiment, he prepared some broth within a special compartment that was completely sealed off from any outside air. Pasteur had already been exploring germ theory and fermentation for some time, so he was already a full believer in germ theory. But if the idea of spontaneous generation was true, then the broth should have been able to spoil even within its air-sealed compartment.

However, Pasteur's guess about spontaneous generation turned out to be correct. When the broth remained sealed, it showed no sign of being impacted by microorganisms. It didn't spoil, instead remaining uncontaminated. But when Pasteur finally broke the seal, the liquid almost instantly started to spoil.

This experiment opened the door to a much greater understanding of how disease happens. Pasteur's work created massive changes in safety standards around food. Once it was known that disease and fermentation happened because of an outside source, it was much easier to work on methods to prevent this. His work eventually led to his discovery of pasteurization. This is a process that has made many products, including wine, eggs, and milk, much safer to consume. Before pasteurization, it was not uncommon to contract serious illnesses due to bacteria in different food products. Raw milk was a particularly vicious culprit.

Today, many countries have laws around pasteurization and the sale of raw milk. While the sale of raw milk in the United States is allowed under certain circumstances, it is under fairly strict regulation, and for good reason. Raw milk can carry salmonella, staph, and listeria, among many other harmful bacteria. A study of illnesses connected to the consumption of raw milk in the United States between the years 1998 and 2018 saw that raw milk was responsible for 202 different outbreaks.

These outbreaks caused 2,645 illnesses and over 200 hospitalizations. It was also found that areas that allowed the sale of raw milk saw over three times the number of outbreaks than areas where the sale of raw milk was prohibited. This study demonstrated the effectiveness of both pasteurization and laws regulating the sale of raw milk.

Pasteurization has evolved since first being developed, and there are two different ways that it is commonly done. In the United States, most milk is pasteurized in a process known as high-temperature short-time pasteurization (HTST). HTST is able to be performed on large quantities of milk at the same time, which is cost-effective and, therefore, an attractive process for dairy producers. However, this type of pasteurization, while still getting rid of bacteria, doesn't have a very long shelf life. It generally needs to be consumed within a few weeks, and it has to be refrigerated to remain safe to drink.

Outside of North America, the most popular form of pasteurization is something called ultra-heat-treated pasteurization, or UHT for short. This pasteurization process heats milk to a higher temperature than is used in HTST, which also results in a slightly different taste than the milk you might be used to drinking in the United States. UHT milk does not need to be refrigerated and can last for three months on the shelf.

This advancement in the understanding of germ theory led to other food safety measures, including the treatment of eggs. Once again, the choice of treatment varies greatly between the North American approach and the approach many European countries and other areas of the world take when it comes to preventing serious foodborne illnesses.

One of the main concerns related to the consumption of eggs is the risk of salmonella. Salmonella contamination is most commonly caused by bacteria that make their way onto an eggshell. This is due to the excess of ground material and feces that are often found in chicken coops and factories. Salmonella might also appear underneath the shell if the laying hen is experiencing an internal infection.

Because of the risk of salmonella, it became common practice in North America for egg producers to put all of their eggs through a vigorous cleaning process as soon as they were laid. This rids the shells of any harmful bacteria and, in theory, makes them safe for consumption.

However, this process does end up causing another potential problem, as it rids the egg of a small protective layer known as a cuticle.

A cuticle is what helps the egg protect itself from bacteria passing through the shell and into the egg, which opens up the possibility of salmonella still being present inside the egg. Because of this, eggs in North America need to be refrigerated, and it is recommended that all eggs be cooked before consumption.

In Europe, there is a law prohibiting the washing of eggs in order to keep that cuticle intact. Eggs are kept on the shelf instead of the fridge. This is to prevent bacteria from forming inside the egg when switching between cold and warm temperatures.

Both methods have seen reductions in foodborne illnesses. However, it's hard to determine if one method is superior. The differences in population numbers make it hard to get comparable studies. Nevertheless, these kinds of changes within food safety can be traced back to the theory that helped discover the bacterium behind the Black Death.

Of course, with any advancement in science, there comes a group of skeptics. When the pasteurization of milk was first suggested in the state of New York, it was met with a fair amount of resistance. It was not until rates of foodborne illnesses dramatically decreased that it began to become widely adopted all over the country.

Even today, there are some groups who claim that pasteurized milk is harmful or less nutritional than raw milk. These claims have generally been made by individuals with no scientific background, and they have all been dismissed by the major health organizations in the United States.

Another area that underwent a major transformation in part because of the Black Death was the healthcare system as a whole. Prior to the Black Death making its way through Europe, a lot of medical professionals operated at an individual level. There was very little oversight, and the idea of regulations put in place for the health of all of society wasn't particularly common.

After the recommendations regarding sanitation measures were made by Edwin Chadwick, cities around the world started reevaluating the way they looked at public health. While the understanding at the time was still focused on the theory of miasma, changes made at this time set the stage for health agencies today.

Health surveys became commonplace. These looked at different areas and measured the rates of diseases within them to help determine what was causing an increase in illness or death within different populations. This is a practice that continues today and is incredibly useful for helping to initiate social change. Health surveys are done through things like the census or by measuring wastewater in different areas to detect rates of disease.

This type of work eventually led to the creation of various health agencies, as well as better oversight and sanitation procedures in hospitals. This, in turn, also helped develop better water management systems, which helped reduce the number of people falling ill from contaminated drinking water.

All of this work spiraled off into other positive advancements in healthcare systems. In the United States, there was an increased interest in funding institutions that were specifically designed to assist individuals who were struggling with their mental health. Before, it had been common to simply shut people with mental health issues in jail, but throughout the late 1800s, many mental health facilities were opened with the express purpose of helping to cope with this issue.

Unfortunately, these early institutions were not particularly helpful. They frequently practiced extremely troubling and ineffective methods, such as electroshock therapy and lobotomies. However, this early separation of mental health institutions from the criminal justice system laid the groundwork for the many transformative and helpful mental health facilities around the world today.

Vinegar and Heat

As you might remember from our chapter on the various cures and treatments people used during the early waves of the Black Death, there were many questionable ingredients. A lot of this was due to the misunderstanding about how exactly the disease was contracted. However, even though the theories behind a few of the methods were incorrect, it turns out that not all of the treatments people tried were useless.

One of the most popular tonics that was applied during the Black Death was the four thieves' vinegar tonic. It was rumored that rubbing it on one's body would prevent the plague from infecting you. This is not entirely true, but there is some validity to vinegar's disinfecting powers.

A study from 2014 found that acetic acid, which is the active ingredient within vinegar, can be an effective killer of mycobacteria. This study was specifically conducted on the bacterium that causes tuberculosis after it had been exposed to acetic acid for thirty minutes.

Although this was an exciting discovery, there are some drawbacks. Vinegar may be effective against certain bacteria, but it is not as powerful and reliable as commercial-grade disinfectants. It also is generally not capable of killing as high a percentage of bacteria as something like bleach. However, its beneficial disinfecting qualities can be of great use to those who may not be in a position to afford commercial products. Vinegar is also less hazardous than other disinfectants, which can sometimes create highly toxic fumes if used incorrectly. (This can also happen with vinegar as well. The combination of vinegar and bleach can quickly create a highly poisonous chlorine gas that can be lethal.)

While vinegar may not be the right choice as a disinfectant everywhere, it certainly has its benefits. During the Black Death, it was often used as a preventative rub as opposed to a cleanser, which might have made it more effective for people hoping to escape the plague. It is very likely that vinegar played a part in helping some people avoid infection, and it's a cheap and effective tool for helping people stay safer from disease today.

Another method that wasn't used correctly but still had some validity to it was the use of fire to dispel or prevent disease. While it was thought that fire would rid a person of disease, the actual benefit behind using heat to combat the plague is that high heat is capable of killing bacteria. That's why it's recommended that you cook something like chicken, which is a common culprit in foodborne illnesses.

Although Pope Clement VI likely avoided the Black Death due to his continual isolation, the constant state of heat in his chambers might have helped protect him from bacteria if anyone else entered the room.

Heat is one of the most effective methods we have against disease today. As you have already learned, pasteurization is a method that uses high heat to prevent bacterial growth. Heat is also a commonly used method for the sterilization of medical equipment. While other methods, such as disinfectants, are used as well, a lot of tools are cleaned using a hot steaming method.

Citizens also use heat to protect themselves every day. People boil water, cook food, and sterilize health products in boiling water to protect themselves from contracting infections. It's a simple, effective, and affordable tool to keep everyone safe.

Although heat is a legitimate method of destroying bacteria, it's important to know the specific requirements of your situation. Depending on what you're trying to clean and what your elevation is, different items need different amounts of time to be considered safe. It is also necessary that food or non-edible items be sanitized in temperatures that are over 149 degrees Fahrenheit. You might be interested to know that this is actually below boiling temperature. However, boiling is often a good measurement to know that you have reached the correct temperature without having to reach for a thermometer.

Epidemiology

In loose terms, epidemiology is the study of the patterns and spread of disease. Throughout history, physicians have sought to find some logic and understanding behind why diseases spread so fast or why some people seem to get sick while others manage to escape an illness.

For a long time, a lot of early epidemiology was tied to guesswork, religion, and observations one could make with the naked eye. It wasn't until the late 1600s that a microscope was created that was powerful enough to see some of the bacteria we now know are responsible for disease.

A major shift in the field of epidemiology came along with Dr. John Snow's discoveries. Because of his findings, it was determined that cholera was spread through contaminated water. Some water in London began to be treated with chlorine, and the rates of cholera decreased.

A few decades after Snow's conclusions surrounding cholera, Joseph Lister began disinfecting medical instruments and a patient's wounds before surgery, which greatly reduced septic shock during medical procedures. This is now standard practice all over the world.

Also in the 1800s were the experiments of Robert Koch. He further supported germ theory by making the discovery that specific germs were responsible for diseases like cholera, anthrax, and tuberculosis.

We have already covered Pasteur's contributions to food safety due to his study of fermentation and work that demonstrated the spontaneous generation theory was incorrect. But there was another major contribution Pasteur made to science and the understanding and prevention of disease: the creation of vaccines.

In the late 1800s, Pasteur was gifted a laboratory by the French government. The lab was given to him in the hopes that he could direct his energy into studying diseases.

At this time, the first vaccination had already taken place, but it hadn't followed the same science that became standard up until a few years ago when RNA vaccines stepped into the spotlight.

For some time, it had been thought that the best way to prevent disease was to purposefully expose yourself to it. Things like "measles parties" have gone in and out of fashion, although they are incorrect ways to protect yourself against disease. While it's true that surviving a disease might potentially provide your body with immunity against it, that still requires you to withstand the initial infection, something that not everyone manages to achieve. Plus, the long-term effects of any kind of infection might be extremely detrimental to one's health.

So, during the 1800s, when it was still thought that exposure might be the best cure, a farmer named Benjamin Jesty began to experiment with cowpox to prevent the contraction of smallpox. At the time, smallpox was a very serious killer, typically leaving 30 percent of those infected dead.

Jesty had previously heard stories about how those who had been infected with cowpox, a skin infection that is common in farm animals, were incapable of contracting smallpox.

Incredibly, without any kind of scientific background, Jesty took it upon himself to purposefully infect his wife and children with a cowpox lesion he had discovered on one of his barnyard animals. Remarkably, this technique proved to be effective and is now generally accepted as the starting point of modern-day vaccines.

It's worth noting that this discovery is often attributed to a physician named Edward Jenner. Jenner did indeed do further testing to confirm that cowpox was effective in combating smallpox infection, but this was done several years later on the basis of Jesty's work.

Years later, when Pasteur started working in the lab, he went back to this first vaccine and decided to dedicate his research to finding vaccines for other diseases. He reasoned that if one had been found for smallpox, then it made sense that all diseases must have something that was a successful combatant against it.

While he initially chose to study a few different forms of disease, he eventually narrowed in on a specific type of cholera that affects chickens. In the beginning, he experimented by purposefully infecting the chickens with live versions of the cholera culture, but after multiple trials, he ended with the same results each time: the chickens would get sick, and many of them would die.

Despite Pasteur's impressive scientific history and incredible genius, one of the best elements of the story of how he found the vaccine is the fact that it happened partly by chance.

After some time experimenting, Pasteur happened to leave town for a few days. When he got back to town, he injected the chickens with the culture as he had many times before, except none of them became sick this time.

While he had been away, the cultures themselves had died, therefore rendering them unable to infect their host. Now, this is where a moment in history was truly created. Pasteur could have, very understandably, assumed that the cultures were useless. Once he realized they were dead, it would have made perfect sense for him to start over with a live culture and continue to go down the wrong path of exploration. However, even though it was clear that he was working with an attenuated culture, he decided to continue experimenting. And he decided to inject the healthy chickens with a live culture of fowl cholera.

What happened next changed everything: the chickens didn't get sick. Pasteur then realized that a harmless version of a bacteria or virus had the potential to protect the immune system from developing infection. In May 1881, he put this to the test in front of a public audience.

Pasteur took an attenuated (weakened or dead) version of anthrax and injected it into sheep, some cows, and a goat. He also had the same amount and distribution of animals who were not injected with the weakened anthrax and used them as the control group in the experiment.

A few weeks later, Pasteur and the audience once again met for the second part of the experiment. This was when Pasteur injected all of the animals with the live bacterium. Just two days later, the ramifications of Pasteur's discovery were clear. All of the control animals were either sick or dead, and all the animals who had been inoculated two weeks earlier were in perfectly good health.

This early success in Pasteur's vaccine experiments led him to work on diseases that also affected humans. He soon created an effective rabies vaccine, and from that point on, public support for vaccine research grew tremendously. Vaccines eventually went on to be developed for a variety of diseases, such as polio, hepatitis A and B, and mumps. The discovery of vaccines changed the course of medical history and has saved countless lives. The yearly flu vaccine that people get all over the world is a result of the development of a vaccine due to the widespread death toll of the 1918 Spanish flu. It is an incredibly important tool for the prevention of disease, and many people consider Pasteur to be a hero.

Discovery of Y. pestis and a Cure for the Black Death

Now, after everything you've learned about the death tolls and the troubling outcomes of the bubonic plague, let's dive into how its cause was discovered and how an effective treatment was eventually developed.

As you may remember from our opening chapter, the origin of the plague was discovered by Alexandre Yersin in 1894. Yersin himself spent some time at the Institut Pasteur, where he spent some time working on vaccine innovation. He and Émile Roux share in the discovery of the diphtheria toxin. However, it is Yersin's discovery of the bacterium responsible for the Black Death for which he is the most famous.

Incredibly, within just two years of Yersin's discovery, an effective antiserum was already being used to treat patients who had become ill with the Black Death. This thorough understanding of the cause of the disease was the true beginning of the end for its hold on the world.

Antiserum, which is a treatment made up of blood that contains the antibodies necessary to fight against the disease, was the standard method for combating the Black Death up until the 1930s when antiserum treatments were replaced by a drug that inhibited the multiplication of *Y. pestis*. Over the next twenty years, further treatments were developed that eventually led to the standard and effective antibiotic treatment that is still used to this day.

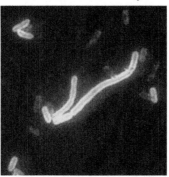

An image of Y. Pestis.
https://commons.wikimedia.org/wiki/File:Yersinia_pestis_fluorescent.jpeg

After Yersin's discovery, a vaccine was also developed to aid in the prevention of the Black Death. Although the vaccines were also effective, they weren't as widely used as some other vaccines. By this point in time, the rates of the plague were already diminishing, and the use of the vaccines was predominantly reserved for soldiers who were serving in areas where there were higher rates of the disease. Today, there is almost no continued use of the Black Death vaccine. Instead, people simply have to take a course of antibiotics to rid themselves of symptoms.

While the plague is treatable today, it can still lead to death if not attended to fast enough. Outcomes are best if antibiotics are prescribed within twenty-four hours of symptoms appearing, so it's very important that anyone who suspects they have contracted the disease gets to a doctor or emergency room immediately.

Today, the United States usually sees around seven cases of the bubonic plague each year. It is typically found in more rural areas, where it may have been passed onto humans by animals. Serious outbreaks of the disease are unlikely thanks to effective treatments, but it's still important that it be taken seriously. If someone can't access or afford treatment, then it could be possible for the disease to spread quickly, so fast treatment must be available for everyone so we can keep the horrors of the Black Death in the past.

While the Black Death was the most destructive pandemic in history, it helped create medical innovations and sanitation systems that have changed the world for the better. Without such a tragic loss of life, there might not have existed the same interest in epidemiology or an insistence on social change. While it was a horrible event that continued for hundreds of years, it arguably changed the world for the better.

Chapter 9: Economic and Social Consequences

The Black Death had enormous economic and social consequences on the lives of people around the world. In Europe, Asia, and North Africa, there was almost no one who had not been impacted by the Black Death. Many of the conversations surrounding the impacts of the Black Death are focused on the economy, such as the changes that happened in the labor market. These are important conversations to have, and we will review the importance of this matter later on in this chapter. However, there is another matter that doesn't always get the attention it deserves: the impact the Black Death had on people's mental health.

It's only very recently that the stigma around mental health has begun to fade away. For a long time, conditions like depression and anxiety, as well as psychiatric disorders, were seen as something embarrassing and shameful. Many people hid their diagnoses or tried to pretend they didn't have them. Thankfully, society is finally starting to talk about mental health issues in earnest. While we still have a long way to go, there is a lot more understanding about mental health than there has ever been.

However, if we are only just now fully beginning to accept the importance of taking care of one's mental health in the year 2023, you can probably imagine what kind of resources might have been available to someone living through an unprecedented pandemic in the year 1337.

To better understand the impact the Black Death had on mental health, let's first look at what trauma does to the brain.

Trauma is defined as a deeply distressing or disturbing experience. Trauma can be a singular event or an ongoing one. While some people might believe that trauma is something that is simply experienced and then let go of, it has been shown that trauma can actually change the chemistry of your brain.

When someone is in a safe environment, they are able to effectively use their prefrontal cortex. This is the planning part of the brain. It helps with rational thought and decision-making. Its smooth operation is crucial to help keep us safe and make logical decisions.

When we experience a traumatic event, the prefrontal cortex is not able to function the way it should. Instead, it goes into a circuit of fear. When the prefrontal cortex is in this mode, it is very difficult for a person to think or act rationally. They might get angry, go numb and shut down, physically run away, or mentally disassociate.

This natural response to trauma can be very difficult for people who have never experienced this phenomenon to understand. It has caused many problems during court cases when victims of physical or sexual attacks take the stand. Often, due to this disruption to a victim's prefrontal cortex, they might not act in the way you think they "should." However, their ability for rational thought was severely compromised due to the trauma they experienced.

Trauma can also have a profound effect on memory. During this state, your brain is not able to process and encode memories the way it normally does, so it is very common for people who've experienced trauma to have a lot of gaps in their recollection of events. Sometimes, entire events will be blank in someone's mind.

Of course, the hope is that someone who has experienced severe trauma is able to access the help they need. However, those kinds of medical professionals were not widely available during the Middle Ages. While therapeutic practices have been documented since ancient Greece, it simply wasn't common practice to receive help for trauma during the Black Death. Plus, with such a drastic loss of life, getting help for even the most basic needs was often a challenge since so many physicians died.

In a paper by Erin Carty, it's discussed how the plague completely altered people's demeanor. The Black Death was such an indiscriminate killer. It didn't matter what your age, race, religion, or economic status was; it came for everyone. This created an enormous sense of panic, paranoia, and hopelessness.

This feeling is evident in the response that many Catholics had toward their church during the pandemic. The church saw a devastating loss of clergymen, which resulted in the institution not being able to see to the needs of all of its members. Some parishes completely shut down, and others were overwhelmed with requests for Mass, funeral ceremonies, and absolution.

Whatever your relationship is with the church, you may expect that Catholics would have had some sympathy for the unprecedented situation in which the church found itself. The loss of life within the church had not been through any fault of its own. In fact, as mentioned earlier, the large number of dead within the church might have been due to the clergy's overexposure to the sick as they attempted to bring their followers some comfort in their final days.

However, compassion was not the response given by many members of the church. Instead, the church was blamed for its lack of numbers and its inability to meet the demands made upon it. Members sought other means of comfort, such as joining the controversial flagellant movement or starting new branches of Christianity. While there were certainly some who must have already been dissatisfied with the church prior to the start of the Black Death, it is interesting to wonder how many would have had such a visceral response to the church's troubles had the entire continent not experienced severe trauma at the same time.

One of the effects that trauma had on the people who lived through the Black Death was an increased preference for isolation. The fear of contracting the disease was so great that being on one's own became the only way some people knew how to survive. This was, of course, exacerbated by the extensive quarantines that people were required to abide by. While quarantines are a necessary preventative measure to limit the spread of disease, they can also have profound impacts on people's mental health. Human beings thrive on connection. Human touch is essential for one's health and happiness. In fact, touch is so important that babies who don't receive enough physical contact from their parents can get sick, have stunted development, or even die.

Some of the people who lived through the pandemic might have also been quarantined with loved ones who died. In some cases, people might have ended up barricaded in their homes with deceased loved ones for weeks. This unimaginable horror adds an almost unbearable weight to an already difficult situation.

People who suffer from trauma can go on to develop a host of mental health issues, such as a dependency on alcohol and sex addiction. Without any resources for treatment back in the day, many people suffered from these issues for the rest of their lives.

Another social consequence that developed out of the trauma of the Black Death was an increase in xenophobia and antisemitism. While we have already touched on the antisemitism that ran rampant during the Black Death, there was also a general distrust and suspicion of immigrants and even people who came from different regions or towns.

When people are scared or angry, they often look for someone to blame. When there is no one person or group who can be held responsible, people often decide to blame whoever seems or looks different than them. So, people began to blame people from other places or people who were in a lower class than they were. This is a pattern that has been repeated throughout history. We've witnessed it very recently with the drastic increase in hate crimes perpetrated against those of Asian descent.

Sadly, this behavior only further contributes to feelings of paranoia and loneliness, but again, many people weren't able to think straight. In difficult times, people search for a sense of control. For some, that might mean helping others, but for many, it means placing blame and pushing people away. It sometimes even results in violence.

People became increasingly protective of their own communities. In some areas of Europe, visitors were required to go through an intensive inspection process, and in some cases, they were not even allowed within city limits. This was especially true of tradesmen, who, while providing an essential service, were often blamed for the spread of the plague.

Nobody experiences trauma in the same way. For some, living through the Black Death made them a better, more compassionate person. It brought them closer to their faith and gave them a renewed appreciation for life. But for many others, it shattered their sense of self and their relationship to the world around them. Many experienced complete breakdowns and completely withdrew from their lives and personal and professional obligations. Some people lost the ability to function and were never again able to regain anything even remotely resembling their former life.

Before we move on to some of the other major changes and consequences of the Black Death, there's something important that should be mentioned: the issue of blame itself. Of course, it's natural to want to understand the origins of something like the Black Death. In fact, doing so is an important part of learning how to prevent something like it from happening again in the future. However, distrusting an entire ethnic group or reacting violently toward others is never an appropriate response.

Rise of Antisemitism

The surge of antisemitism and authorities' response to it set a dangerous precedent for the years to come. Instances of antisemitism had already been growing across Europe prior to the start of the pandemic, but it increased dramatically once the disease took hold.

As has already been mentioned, many people simply used the Black Death as an excuse to scapegoat the Jewish community and enact their hatred without consequence. And for many, there were no consequences for their actions.

While some authorities spoke out against the mistreatment and killing of Jews, there were many others who stood idly by. Sometimes, government officials and church leaders would even encourage the attacks.

In a study conducted by Finley and Koyama, it was found that attacks on the Jewish community were much more severe in cities that were governed by Catholic leaders. In those cities, Jews were often killed in extremely high numbers. Sometimes, their population would be completely eliminated.

Cities that were ruled by a secular leader saw much lower persecution rates, which speaks loudly to the vendetta the Catholics had against the Jews.

This general ambivalence or blatant encouragement of the massacre of the Jewish people set the stage for future antisemitic attacks. Left unchecked, this eventually led to the attempted genocide of the Jewish people by the Nazis in World War II. By the end of the war, six million Jews had been murdered.

During the most recent pandemic, the same lie was spread regarding the Jewish community, that they had somehow designed and spread the disease with the aim of growing their own population. Since then, the world has observed a spike in antisemitic hate crimes. Despite our incredible access to world events and history, we seem to be continually doomed to repeat our past mistakes. That's why it's so important to continue to learn and spread knowledge.

Inflation and Labor

As is common with most pandemics, the aftermath saw increased rates of inflation. The stalling of every trade system made goods much more difficult and expensive to acquire, and the loss of workers also made the cost of labor go up. This created intense frustration for the upper class, but the higher cost of labor eventually ended up changing the fabric of society.

Europe had previously operated under a feudal system, with a clear separation between lords and their serfs. Higher pay suddenly raised many former peasants to a different level of society, and the middle class was born.

As more and more people began to make a decent living, there was a surge in demand for products that might have been unattainable to laborers before. Even with inflation, people were eager to spend their hard-earned money. After all, there had been very little to celebrate for many years, and in between waves of the plague, people did their best to enjoy what life had to offer.

The creation of the middle class was instrumental in helping the economy recover, as well as providing a better quality of life to a large part of the population. Had the Black Death not happened, there is no telling how long the feudal system might have remained in place.

For a long time, the middle class was a level of wealth that many people aspired to enjoy. This was because people in the middle class generally lived comfortable and happy lives. It was common for people in the middle class to secure a comfortable job and be able to afford a home and the occasional comfort or indulgence.

The middle class expanded for many years. In the 1970s, adults in the middle class in the United States sat at 61 percent. However, over the last twenty years, that number has fallen. The percentage sat at 50 percent in 2021. Of course, this means that the upper class has grown, but it also means the lower class has expanded as well.

A stark divide between the upper and lower classes is a phenomenon that has happened in other countries around the world as well.

Currently, there are several attacks on unions and labor protections and regulations all over the world. Many people have to hold several jobs to make ends meet and are being priced out of major cities. Steady, tenured jobs are often being replaced by gig work with no stability or pensions. However, a lot of the massive labor changes that took place after the first wave of the Black Death took several years, in some cases decades, to organize. Looking back at what happened in the 1300s can perhaps shine a light on what the future might hold for us.

Safety

One thing is certain: The Black Death made the world a safer place. The extreme nature of the disease forced authorities to make massive changes to the way buildings, cities, and healthcare facilities were designed. It also helped create many safe food practices and water purification systems.

Of course, these advancements were not all a direct result of the Black Death, but many of the investigations and experiments that led to these advancements began because of a desperate desire to stem the spread of the plague. These changes to society not only improved the quality of life for survivors but also extended it. And these changes continued to improve over time. Today, many of us are privileged to live in cities that have advanced systems to treat and process food and water. We also have state-of-the-art laboratories, hospitals, and schools that are constantly working to better understand infectious diseases so that we can catch and deal with them as soon as they appear.

Politics

The final area that we'll cover in this chapter is how the Black Death changed politics.

When the Black Death drastically affected the labor market, it meant there was also a shift in the political landscape. Before the arrival of the bubonic plague, many of the lowest-earning members of society had been disenfranchised and did not have much power in the political system.

While political systems might have remained fairly unchanged in areas that didn't experience extremely high death tolls, there was a dramatic shift in areas that had. This created a shift in labor and introduced the middle class. These newly elevated members of society suddenly had a voice in politics and were able to take positions of power, as well as vote for officials that they actually felt would act in their best interest. Prior to the Black Death, politics had been controlled by the elite members of the upper class, who, of course, worked hard to continue the exploitative practices of the feudal system.

This shift in politics created a stronger balance between opposing views and eventually led to party systems, which are common in many countries all over the world today.

In an interview with Gingerich and Vogler, it was discussed how political change was much slower in regions that hadn't experienced high death tolls. Feudal systems were more rigorously protected in these areas, and voter suppression among conservative leaders ran rampant. Land inequality in areas with a lot of loss greatly diminished, and the overall quality of life for everyone in those areas improved.

Of course, these researchers considered the obvious differences in loss of life in different areas due to density differences between rural and urban situations. In general, it was common for rural areas to have better outcomes when it came to deaths simply because there were fewer people to spread the disease. Rural areas had a more dispersed population, which meant better ventilation and pre-established social distancing. However, the trade-off for these areas seemed to be that they took longer to catch up to positive social and economic changes after the first wave of the plague died down.

Despite the fact that some regions progressed more slowly than others, it is an indisputable fact that the Black Death changed the face of politics forever.

There are numerous social and economic changes that happened as a result of the Black Death. Some have been extensively studied, while others have been lost and forgotten to time. Once again, these issues provide a valuable lesson from which we can hopefully learn in order to prevent the same mistakes from happening in the future.

Conclusion

No one wants to imagine the worst-case scenario. The Black Death was a horrific event that permanently changed the course of history. There are so many people who never got to live out their dreams because of this disease. Who knows what art, scientific discoveries, and social advancements we might have had so much earlier had the Black Death never happened. But there's another valid question to ask that's the opposite of that. How much later would we have had some of these things if it hadn't happened?

Would there have been such an intense interest in bacteria and the origin of disease if the Black Death hadn't happened? Would democracy be the same if it hadn't happened? Would we still be operating under a feudal system?

While some of these questions may seem laughable, they are not entirely ridiculous. In this book, there have been several examples of how history has repeated itself after similar traumas, even though there are so many resources that detail how those same choices ended before. Sometimes, the only thing that can really shake up a society and create meaningful change is a catastrophic event like the bubonic plague.

That's not to say that a pandemic is the only way to change the status quo. There have been many movements throughout history that have managed to change long-entrenched social systems through grassroots organizations and a strong passion for the cause. But it's undeniable that the Black Death resulted in some major positive changes.

Even now, many populations around the world, including the United States, live within a system that is predominantly controlled by a wealthy few. Those in the highest tax bracket generally hold the most powerful positions in politics, control think tanks and global corporations, and control the cost of living and wages. Is it a stretch to imagine that some of these politicians and CEOs might comfortably operate within a feudal system if given the chance?

And what would healthcare look like today without the impact of the Black Death? Although there were several other diseases that caused widespread death, there was nothing as severe as the bubonic plague. Is it possible that the loss of life from other ailments wouldn't have been deemed devastating enough to initiate further investigation?

Without the discovery of germ theory, we might still be sitting beside sewage in the hopes of warding off disease. That might not be difficult because we might still be throwing our waste onto the street. Again, this might seem silly and a bit difficult to imagine, but remember that humans can be slow to change and often repeat previous mistakes. Looking back at the 1918 Spanish flu pandemic, it might seem impossible that anyone would have negative reactions to basic public health measures, which people resisted back then. And the same argument appeared again about one hundred years later.

The Black Death showed us that pandemics are quick to fuel animosity and hatred. They stoke powerlessness and hopelessness, and people often turn to anger and extremist views when faced with these feelings. The long history of this pattern can help us learn how to have more measured responses to tragic events such as this. Because another thing the Black Death has taught us is that pandemics will keep on coming. However, it's up to us to decide how we respond to them.

The fear and isolation that happen as a result of a pandemic is detrimental to our health and society at large. In order to create a better world, we need to move forward to embrace curiosity and compassion because there usually is something better on the other side.

Here's another book by Enthralling History that you might like

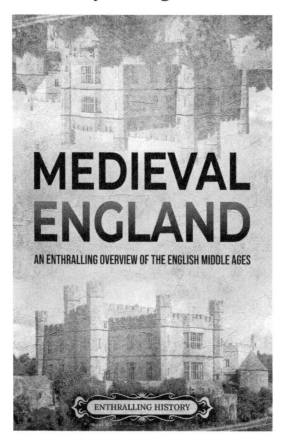

Free limited time bonus

Stop for a moment. We have a free bonus set up for you. The problem is this: we forget 90% of everything that we read after 7 days. Crazy fact, right? Here's the solution: we've created a printable, 1-page pdf summary for this book that you're reading now. All you have to do to get your free pdf summary is to go to the following website:

https://livetolearn.lpages.co/enthrallinghistory/

Once you do, it will be intuitive. Enjoy, and thank you!

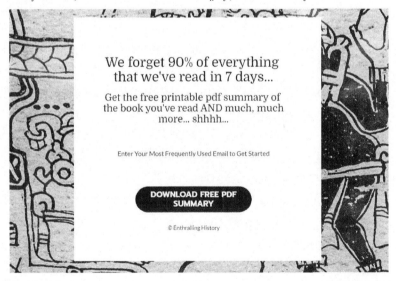

We forget 90% of everything
that we've read in 7 days...

Get the free printable pdf summary of
the book you've read AND much, much
more... shhhh...

Enter Your Most Frequently Used Email to Get Started

**DOWNLOAD FREE PDF
SUMMARY**

© Enthralling History

Bibliography

- https://study.com/learn/lesson/the-four-humors-blood-phlegm-black-bile-yellow-bile.html
- https://www.folger.edu/blogs/shakespeare-and-beyond/the-four-humors-eating-in-the-renaissance/
- https://curiosity.lib.harvard.edu/contagion/feature/humoral-theory
- http://exhibits.usu.edu/exhibits/show/bookofsecretes/medicine
- https://www.tehrantimes.com/news/415195/Sanguine-temperament-Specifications-and-lifestyle
- https://www.worldhistory.org/article/1540/medieval-cures-for-the-black-death/
- https://bcmj.org/premise/history-bloodletting
- https://www.popularmechanics.com/science/a32759535/newton-toad-vomit-plague-cure/
- https://www.sciencedirect.com/science/article/pii/S0378874121007649
- https://www.wondriumdaily.com/how-the-church-handled-the-black-death-in-the-14th-century/
- https://www.oxfordreference.com/display/10.1093/oi/authority.20110803100046308;jsessionid=8FE8751E77C563B813D981AD9A6BA156

- https://www.businessinsider.com/labor-shortage-history-black-death-plague-king-pay-increase-serfdom-2021-12
- https://www.historic-uk.com/HistoryUK/HistoryofEngland/Wat-Tyler-the-Peasants-Revolt/
- https://www.wondriumdaily.com/how-the-church-handled-the-black-death-in-the-14th-century/
- https://artincontext.org/black-death-art/
- https://www.montana.edu/historybug/yersiniaessays/medrano.html#:~:text=The%20trauma%20of%20the%20Black,then%20poetized%2C%20and%20finally%20painted.
- https://momentmag.com/why-were-jews-blamed-for-the-black-death/
- https://www.worldhistory.org/article/1541/religious-responses-to-the-black-death/
- https://www.britannica.com/event/Western-Schism
- https://www.historicmysteries.com/avignon-captivity/
- https://www.britannica.com/event/Avignon-papacy
- https://jewishreviewofbooks.com/articles/9866/jews-genes-and-the-black-death/#
- https://historyinnumbers.com/events/black-death/flagellants/#:~:text=October%201349%20%E2%80%93%20the%20month%20that,as%20Shi'a%20Islam).
- https://source.colostate.edu/penance-and-plague-how-the-black-death-changed-one-of-christianitys-most-important-rituals/
- http://web.stanford.edu/class/history13/Readings/MichaelDol.htm#:~:text=The%20Muslim%20reaction%20to%20the,mass%20funerals%20in%20the%20mosques.
- https://knowledge.uchicago.edu/record/3111?ln=en
- https://egrove.olemiss.edu/cgi/viewcontent.cgi?article=1682&context=hon_thesis
- https://www.worldhistory.org/article/1541/religious-responses-to-the-black-death/

- https://www.crf-usa.org/bill-of-rights-in-action/bria-26-2-the-black-death-a-catastrophe-in-medieval-europe.html#:~:text=The%20Response%20of%20Religion%20and,medical%20schools%20existed%20in%20Europe.

- https://www.ncbi.nlm.nih.gov/pmc/articles/PMC9949692/

- https://academic.oup.com/jsh/article/45/3/809/1746067

- https://www.history.com/news/quarantine-black-death-medieval

- https://time.com/5799525/coronavirus-covid19-quarantine-ships-history/

- https://bigthink.com/health/what-ended-the-black-death-historys-worst-pandemic/#:~:text=The%20eventual%20weakening%20of%20the,slowing%20the%20plague's%20terror%20march.

- https://www.history.com/news/pandemics-end-plague-cholera-black-death-smallpox

- https://www.britannica.com/biography/Sir-John-Pringle-1st-Baronet

- https://health.mil/News/Articles/2021/07/01/Evolution-MHS-MSMR

- https://www.wearewater.org/en/sewage-the-trace-of-our-history_281141

- https://taras.org/2020/10/10/a-short-history-of-solid-waste-management/#:~:text=Centuries%20with%20no%20organized%20waste,garbage%20was%20a%20common%20practice.

- https://education.nationalgeographic.org/resource/natural-selection/

- https://www.nih.gov/news-events/nih-research-matters/how-black-death-shaped-human-evolution#:~:text=Researchers%20identified%20genetic%20variants%20that,increasing%20susceptibility%20to%20autoimmune%20diseases.

- https://journals.sagepub.com/doi/full/10.1177/18344909211034257

- https://sphweb.bumc.bu.edu/otlt/mph-modules/ph/publichealthhistory/publichealthhistory7.html

- https://www.thelancet.com/journals/lancet/article/PIIS0140-6736(15)61231-4/fulltext
- https://www.britannica.com/topic/feudalism
- https://egrove.olemiss.edu/cgi/viewcontent.cgi?article=1682&context=hon_thesis#:~:text=When%20the%20Black%20Death%20struck%20Europe%20in%201347%2C%20the%20increasingly,its%20vulnerability%20to%20Christian%20society.https://dc.cod.edu/cgi/viewcontent.cgi?article=1657&context=essai#:~:text=The%20Greek%20physician%20Hippocrates%20(c,pestilence%20(Sterner%2C%201).
- https://www.livescience.com/2497-black-death-changed-world.html
- https://www.thehealthy.com/food/why-europeans-dont-refrigerate-eggs/
- https://www.cdc.gov/foodsafety/rawmilk/rawmilk-outbreaks.html
- https://blog.smartsense.co/louis-pasteur-pasteurization
- https://www.britannica.com/story/louis-pasteurs-contributions-to-science#:~:text=Pasteur's%20work%20with%20microorganisms%20in,of%20the%20body%20by%20microorganisms.
- https://www.ncbi.nlm.nih.gov/pmc/articles/PMC3940030/#:~:text=Acetic%20acid%20(vinegar)%20is%20an,disinfectant%20capacity%20of%20organic%20acids.
- https://bio.libretexts.org/Bookshelves/Microbiology/Microbiology_(Boundless)/10%3A_Epidemiology/10.01%3A_Principles_of_Epidemiology/10.1A%3A_History_of_Epidemiology
- https://www.thelancet.com/journals/lancet/article/PIIS0140-6736(06)69878-4/fulltext
- https://www.cdc.gov/vaccines/vpd/vaccines-diseases.html
- https://www.who.int/news-room/spotlight/history-of-vaccination/a-brief-history-of-vaccination#:~:text=Dr%20Edward%20Jenner%20created%20the,cowpox%20were%20immune%20to%20smallpox.&text=In%20May%201796%2C%20English%20physician,the%20hand%2

0of%20a%20milkmaid.

- https://www.vbivaccines.com/evlp-platform/louis-pasteur-attenuated-vaccine/
- https://sciencehistory.org/education/scientific-biographies/louis-pasteur/#:~:text=During%20the%20mid%2D%20to%20late,cholera%2C%20anthrax%2C%20and%20rabies.
- https://www.sciencefocus.com/the-human-body/epidemiology-a-timeline-of-discoveries/
- https://www.aaas.org/discovery-bacteria#:~:text=Two%20men%20are%20credited%20today,discovery%20of%20bacteria%20in%201676.
- https://curiosity.lib.harvard.edu/contagion/feature/germ-theory
- https://www.pasteur.fr/en/research-journal/news/alexandre-yersin-man-who-discovered-bacterium-responsible-plague
- https://www.cnn.com/2020/08/19/health/bubonic-plague-2020-california-wellness/index.html
- https://www.healthline.com/health-news/seriously-dont-worry-about-the-plague#Heres-how-the-plague-spreads
- https://www.nature.com/articles/s41586-022-04800-3
- https://www.science.org/content/article/gene-helped-people-survive-black-death-come-haunt#:~:text=The%20team%20identified%20an%20astonishing,called%20endoplasmic%20reticulum%20aminopeptidase%202.
- https://www.sciencedirect.com/science/article/pii/S1198743X14608582
- https://www.ncbi.nlm.nih.gov/books/NBK218224/
- https://www.unco.edu/assault-survivors-advocacy-program/learn_more/neurobiology_of_trauma.aspx#:~:text=When%20someone%20experiences%20a%20traumatic,all%20have%20inside%20of%20us.
- https://www.wvdhhr.org/birth23/raunewsletters/RAU7_Summer2018_PPNewsletter.pdf

- https://pdxscholar.library.pdx.edu/cgi/viewcontent.cgi?article=1 197&context=younghistorians#:~:text=The%20absence%20of% 20reassurance%20that,on%20the%20function%20of%20society.

- https://jogh.org/2022/jogh-12-03015

- https://www.pewresearch.org/short-reads/2022/04/20/how-the-american-middle-class-has-changed-in-the-past-five-decades/

- https://www.khanacademy.org/humanities/whp-origins/era-5-the-first-global-age/52-old-world-webs-betaa/a/read-trade-networks-and-the-black-death-beta

- https://www.brown.edu/Departments/Italian_Studies/dweb/plag ue/effects/social.php#:~:text=Since%20it%20was%20so%20diffi cult,the%20new%20rise%20in%20wages.

- https://www2.gwu.edu/~iiep/assets/docs/papers/2020WP/Jedwa bIIEP2020-14.pdf

- https://www.ohchr.org/en/press-releases/2020/04/rise-antisemitic-hatred-during-covid-19-must-be-countered-tougher-measures

- https://news.virginia.edu/content/qa-new-research-reveals-political-changes-wrought-black-death

- https://www.ncbi.nlm.nih.gov/books/NBK218224/

- https://www.ncbi.nlm.nih.gov/pmc/articles/PMC3559034/

- https://www.history.com/news/quarantine-black-death-medieval#

- https://www.sciencemuseum.org.uk/objects-and-stories/medicine/bubonic-plague-first-pandemic

- https://education.nationalgeographic.org/resource/silk-road/

- https://www.worldhistory.org/article/1540/medieval-cures-for-the-black-death/

- https://www.nytimes.com/2022/06/15/health/black-death-plague.html#:~:text=Historians%20traced%20the%20epidemic' s%20path,Africa%20and%20the%20Middle%20East.

- https://www.nationalgeographic.com/history/article/plague-doctors-beaked-masks-coronavirus

Printed in Great Britain
by Amazon

31774696R00056